DEEP LEARNING

Beginner's Guide to Learn the Realms of Deep Learning from A-Z

⋝ ROB STEPHEN ⋜

Table of Contents

Introduction

Introduction to Deep Learning

The most common terms in today' s world are "**Artificial Intelligence**," "**Machine Learning,**" and "**Deep Learning.**" Most of these words are used interchangeably. But is it correct? Do all these terms have the same meaning and significance in today's digitally growing world? The answer is NO. The three signify three different sets of learning and are three broad categories that need to be studied and researched individually.

Artificial Intelligence

AI is a way of making a computer think similarly as a human can think and process real-world problems. It uses the human tendency to learn how a human thinks, learns and works while trying to solve day to day life issues. The analysis is then used to develop intelligent software systems.

Artificial intelligence is the superset of all advances that empower PCs to copy human insight. Using the rationale of if-then standards, a decision tree is a machine learning algorithm included in deep learning. Any kind of technology which enables human intelligence in computers is known as artificial intelligence.

Machine Learning

Machine Learning is a subset of Artificial Intelligence. It uses the AI concept, which enables the computer to learn things without being programmed by any human. Based on the output and the success rates it encounters daily, it aligns its activity according to that. It observes the daily success patterns and makes better decisions to attain its aim according to the success pattern.

Machine learning is, therefore, a subset of artificial intelligence in which machine they get improved kind of decision-making experience depending upon the training or the data they have, and it is based upon deep learning. Deep learning is also a part of machine learning.

Deep Learning

Deep Learning can be considered to be a subset of Machine Learning. It depends on the study of the data representations. There is a difference between Machine Learning and Deep Learning. Machine Learning involves parsing the data and produce informed decisions on the basis of the analyzed data, whereas Deep Learning involves creating the neural network (like the neurons in any human body) which will learn and make intelligent decisions on their own without any human interventions.

Deep learning is the subset of Machine Learning, which consists of various highly specialized algorithms that allow the application software to train itself to perform specialized tasks such as image and speech recognition. It is done by exposing the multi-layered networks to a huge amount of data and information.

Deep learning has been successfully implemented in many interesting applications, like autonomous vehicles and real-time translation. Also, it was tried in Google's Deep Learning based on AlphaGo, but the business applications are not just for this purpose. It is used for more immediate impact and is potentially more useful.

Deep Learning is not an overnight success; it became popular after 2010 when it was presented that deep models can be trained using GPUs and activation functions, which will provide better gradient flow. Deep learning is now possible and popular because of the availability of large datasets, availability of GPU(s) for computation, and new Machine Learning methods.

Architecture

Deep neural networks with various hidden layers are capable of sequentially learning the highly complex and specialized features from input pixels of images.

- The first hidden layer will be used for learning the patterns present in local edges.

- All the middle layers will be used for learning the highly specialized and complex features.

- The final layer will be used for classifying the object present in image pixels. That can be anything from an animal to a bird.

Deep Learning Models

Deep Neural Networks (DNN)_– DNN is an artificial neural network (ANN) which has multiple hidden layers between input and output layers. Complex non-linear relationships can be modeled using DNN.

Recurrent Neural Networks (RNN) – In RNN, connections between nodes form a directed graph, i.e., data can flow in any direction in a sequence. When we have a series of data, we will use RNN. RNNs can be used in NLP, Time series prediction, handwriting recognition, speech recognition, etc.

Convolutional Deep Neural Networks (CNN) – It aims to learn higher-order features in the data via convolutions. Most useful when there is some structure to data like in audios and images. It works best for problems like image recognition, object classification. It is used in natural language translation and sentiment analysis.

How to Train Neural Network

- Get a broad set of data. Divide the dataset into Train, Validation, and Test data; let's say into 60:20:20 ratio.

- We will pass the training dataset to our model to extract features and learn from the output. To evaluate the model, we will now pass the validation dataset to it and get the predictions.

- We will then compare the predicted output with the actual output of validation data and measure the accuracy. As per the accuracy level, we can tweak our model, like changing the activation function, number of layers, etc.

- Training a model implies that we are learning from the provided dataset considering the weights and biases present.

Test and Validate Neural Network

- If we evaluate our model multiple times on the test dataset, then we might have a problem of Overfitting. To avoid that, we have divided our dataset into three parts: Train, Validation, and Test.

- We will evaluate our model on the validation dataset and accordingly change the model.

- Once we found a good performing model, we will test our model on the test dataset, which will be unseen before by our model.

Activation Features

Sigmoid – Non-linear function, continuously differentiable. The function ranges from 0-1 having an S shape. (Vanishing gradient problem))

TanH – Quite similar to sigmoid. A scaled version of the sigmoid. It is symmetric over origin. Range -1 to 1. It solves the problem of the values, all being of the same sign. (Vanishing gradient problem)

ReLU – Rectified Linear Unit. Most used, non- linear, it doesn't activate all neurons at the same time (for negative values -> convert to 0 and no activation of neurons). The gradient is 0 for x<0. ReLU function should only be used in the hidden layers

Leaky ReLU - Instead of defining the Relu function as 0 for x less than 0, we define it as a small linear component of x. Replace the horizontal line of ReLU with a non-zero non-horizontal line to remove the gradient.

Softmax – Type of sigmoid, used in classification problem.

Current Application Areas of Deep Learning

- Computer Vision
- NLP
- Speech Recognition
- Drug design
- Board Games
- Bioinformatics – Drug discovery and toxicology

Note: Different application areas use a different type of DL models. For example - images use CNN, text, or speech use RNN.

Real-Life Examples

- Netflix's famous movie recommendation system.
- Winning presidential elections.
- Facial feature detection in SnapChat and Instagram.
- Cancer detection.
- Language translation.
- Playing Go.

- Colorization of Black and White Images.

- Adding Sounds to Silent Movies.

- Automatic Handwriting Generation.

- Financial Fraud detection.

- Facebook's automatically tagging uploaded pictures.

Problems Faced in Deep Learning

- Need for Data - Labeled data is expensive to collect, and without it, DL algorithms don't work so well.

- Expensive - It involves a massive number of computations, so if the dataset is large, you need costly GPUs to speed up the training.

- Interpretability - It is low as compared to other ML models. DL models are like a black box to the user.

- The problem of Generalization – Model trained on train dataset might not perform very well on unseen data.

- Overfitting - Because of added layers of abstraction.

Getting Started

- Install Python with Anaconda Navigator in your machine.

- Open Jupyter Notebook, which is available in Anaconda Navigator.

- Install "Tensor Flow" and "Keras" libraries using 'conda' or 'pip' package managers from anaconda prompt:

- pip install keras

- pip3 install --upgrade tensorflow # for python 3.*

- Keras is high –level neural network library which we use for fast experimentation. It is built on top of TensorFlow and supports CNN, RNN, and both.

Testing with the Help of Deep Learning

Here we will explain Deep Learning and how it makes an impact on testing. Talking in a broader sense, we can think of AI to be a bigger set and machine learning to be a subset of AI and deep learning to be a subset of machine learning. So AI is a bigger set, and deep learning is smallest and machine learning comes in between two.

History of Artificial Intelligence

Artificial intelligence actually came into the picture in the early fifties and sixties. It was mostly about enabling machines to do things on their own in programming machines which later increased into something like robotics and then in early 90s till 2010 we had this machine learning coming into picture where so many different kinds of algorithms and approaches and different kind of theories were discovered and rented to begin machine to start learning on their own and then from 2010 onwards a new field which is a subset of artificial intelligence and machine learning is the subset of artificial intelligence, and deep learning is a subset of machine learning which started in early 2010.

Machine Learning

So what exactly is machine learning? We have a set of training data like we have training sets in which different kinds of data.

Different companies can use data to figure out what they can know, your exact schedule. They can know about your preferences, your choices, your pattern of behavior, and what exactly is your thought process. So depending upon this is application keep on collecting all those data and if that data goes into a hand of some kind of organization. They can do a lot of predictive analysis; they can do a lot of data analysis and applying unsupervised and supervised machine learning. Kind of concept they can go ahead and figure out many decisions which you are you're planning to do or which you think you will take you will do, and depending on those decisions, they can know those decisions in advance.

It is like predicting the future. The companies would already know what kind of decision you are going to take any given certain situations. If certain parameters, they are provided to you what would be your reaction because they know in the past you have done something like this and you have a set of data

Your data is with them that whenever you enter into such kind of environment, you do certain kinds of actions, and companies can predict it, and this is what is done as a part of machine learning, where data is provided feature extraction takes place. Then a predictive model is calculated, and this predictive model is then rolled out for the users for which data was taken.

Now, these are different kinds of areas where machine learning is so much impactful, and it is so much so very much applicable. Areas where machine learning is getting more and more involved nowadays

Machine learning has isolated into three distinct methodologies:

Supervised Learning

In supervised learning, you have classification. So when we talk about classification, image classification, identity classification, identity detection, customer retention, diagnostic all these approaches they use classification technique and the supervised learning of machine learning and then similarly advertising popularity prediction with the forecasting market forecasting estimating the life expectancy population growth prediction all these things they come under duration of supervised learning and the machine learning.

As per this methodology, the code is programmed in such a way that the previous training examples are taken for reference. The previous examples are taken as reference by the program to make the correct decision for the new set of data. So basically, the code is supervised previously to attain the aim.

Unsupervised Learning

Things come under dimension reduction of unsupervised learning, and then you have a second approach, which is known as a cluster. Recommender system, targeted marketing, and customer segmentation, they come and they're part of clustering. All these approaches use the clustering mechanism of unsupervised learning.

As per this methodology, the code is not programmed in any way to get the desired results. A huge bunch of data and must find patterns, and their relationships are defined which helps in deciding the approach without any human intervention.

Reinforcement Learning

Under reinforcement learning, the kind of approaches to machine learning what are developed can be utilized for gaming. Artificial intelligence is skill acquisition learning tasks, robot navigation, and real-time decisions. So these are a different kind of right now in the current industry. Current scenario these are the different practical implementations of machine learning and different techniques of machine learning in different aspects of human life.

Supervised versus Unsupervised Learning

What exactly is supervised learning?

Supervised learning is when a machine learning task learns a function that uses examples of input and output pairs to learn how to map inputs to outputs. Each of the examples consists of one input object and an output value that we want – this is also known as a supervisory signal. Examples of supervised learning include neural networks, support vector machines (SVMs), decision trees, etc.

And unsupervised learning?

This is self-organized learning, a style of Hebbian learning that finds data patterns that were previously unknown and without using pre-existing labels. Unsupervised learning makes use of cluster analysis to group datasets that share attributes to pull out algorithmic relationships.

AI and It's Testing

What is Artificial Intelligence?

These days AI is common across every industrial sector. So, let's discuss what that actually means and how it is widely populous across the world. The Father of Artificial Intelligence, who is named as John McCarthy, defined AI as "The productive usage of science and engineering concepts in developing intelligent computer programs."

Artificial intelligence is designed to behave in the way of robot controlling a computer without human interference by developing software to think alike to that of a human.

As per the analysis made, there are different ways to accomplish Artificial Intelligence by conducting a study on how human's actions would be while performing the tasks as below:

- Thinking
- Learning
- Deciding
- Working
- Trying to solve a problem

- Study of outcomes

- Developing intelligent software

Artificial Intelligence Goals

- Intelligent behavior, learn, demonstrate, and explain aspects to be unveiled by expert Systems Creation thereby directing its users.

- Think, learn, understand, and enact as humans with the machines implemented using Human Intelligence implementation.

Artificial intelligence comprises of science and technology involving a wide variety of concepts such as below are considered as functions of AI to match human intelligence:

- Computer Science

- Psychology

- Voice and speech recognition

- Natural science

- Robotics

- Biology

- Networking

- Linguistics

- Mathematics

- Engineering

- Reasoning

- Learning

- Problem-solving skills

Techniques Used for AI

AI techniques are a way to systematically arrange and make use of the knowledge coherently in such a way that it should be −

- Clear by the people who provide it.

- Easy and malleable to correct errors.

Also, the speed of execution of a complex program can be improvised with AI techniques.

Usage of AI

AI has been widely in use in various fields such as:

Gaming − Games like chess, poker, etc. which are most populous online games make use of AI and design machines, which can determine the huge number of combinations on the basis of experimental problem-solving knowledge.

Vision Systems − Visual input on the computer can be understood, elucidated, and envisaged by these types of systems by making use of AI. Let us take an example as below -

- A spying airplane designed to take photographs to get the map information

- The clinical expert system used by doctors to diagnose patient disease.

- Computer software used by police to identify the face of criminals matching the existing portraits in the system.

Natural Language Processing – With AI, one can interact with the computer in the languages spoken by human beings.

Speech Recognition – Nowadays Voice and speech recognition in search, Siri (in IPhones) are predominantly used and becoming more useful during emergencies also. These systems are designed to handle different types of accents and ignore the background noise.

Handwriting Recognition – Stylus is used to read the text written on paper by a pen using Handwriting recognition software. This can help identify the shapes of the letters and novice it into educable text.

Intelligent Robots –Robots are being designed in such a way that they are able to carry out any kind of human activity with ease and perfection as per the coded program and sensors in the chips are used to detect physical characteristics in the robots such as temperature, light, movement, heat, bump, pressure, and sound. These sensors are designed to work with qualified processors, distinctive sensors, and big memory to represent intelligence.

Term "Robot" has come to use in the year 1923, where Karel Capek first used this term in English. From then on, AI has been growing and making progress in technology by having Interactive robots available commercially to users by 2000. Gaming has wide usage, which is making most out of the market, and IT with AI programming skills are in demand.

Intelligence can also be categorized into different ways as below.

- Musical intelligence

- Linguistic intelligence

- Spatial intelligence

- Logical-mathematical intelligence

- Intra-personal intelligence

- Bodily-Kinesthetic intelligence

- Interpersonal intelligence

Intelligence is composed of Reasoning, Learning, Problem Solving, Perception, and Linguistic Intelligence.

Though there is a difference between how machine intelligence and human intelligence works, especially concerning object recognition, most of the sectors are yielding huge benefits with machine effort using AI than human power these days in Automobiles such as BMW newly launched with AI, etc. Artificial Intelligence is going to be the future of technology in the coming years.

Testing means applying certain kinds of inputs, doing some kind of process, and finding output and if the output is as per the expected behavior, then we will say our tests are passing this is known as software testing.

What is software testing using artificial intelligence? We do the same kind of thing wherein we have input, we have an earlier beam wherein we provide different kinds of data parameters, and then we have a hidden layer that does a different kind of processing of data.

For example, in supervised learning, we had information from the past, and then we compared the new data depending upon the past and figured out a status compared or is processed in terms of the other training data, and then we figure out the decision-making process and try to this or come up with the output.

In unsupervised learning, we don't have anything data, and we collect the data on our own depending on a different kind of situation, depending on different kinds of parameters. We figure out our own way; we figure out our own learning, and then we come up with a decision, which is output.

So it is same, we have set of input, and some actions are taken or some algorithm which does the kind of processing and then we have output and this output if I the expected output is equal to the actual behavior then we statistic passing if actual and expected behavior the test pass and If at all there is an interference then the tests are failing, and we report it as bug this is what is software testing using artificial intelligence.

Why AI in Testing?

Why are artificial intelligence and machine learning going to be so much involved in software testing and software development? Why do we need it? Kind of application what we used to have let's say

20 years back and now the kind of application we used to have are the same? Absolutely not.

We see so many good applications nowadays. We see so many implementations which are so high standard nowadays, which are doing so many different kinds of things and functions for us and which has been all these applications have made our life so easy.

The only thing which is required is this should be high standard quality-wise and performance wise and how can it be ensured it can be ensured by testing. With increasing features, the complexity increases exponentially. That's a proven fact whenever you have a new feature or enhanced feature coming into the picture. The complex simple things are not very complex, and they are very easy to test, but whenever we have some complexity coming into the picture, the new features coming into the picture, the complexity increases exponentially and new features they have a lot and lot of features to be tested.

So this coverage should also increase exponentially, but it cannot take it cannot happen if you're testing manually or if you're testing it using some normal standard procedures, which used to use for testing the earlier application and even for the enhanced or high-level application you're trying to use the same kind of testing mechanism that is not going to work they'll always be a coverage gap.

So within a given point of time, you want to increase the complexity you want to increase the feature, but at the same time in given time, your coverage is not going to increase if you are going to follow the same kind of testing activities and you're going to follow the same testing process in technology.

Hence there is certain need of high-level technology in testing as well, and this is why we have artificial intelligence and machine learning coming into pictures when we talk about software development and testing and to increase the coverage and to cover maximum number of test cases to figure out everything has been covered at this depth we do need artificial intelligence and machine learning.

Chapter 1

GUI Testing Using Deep Learning

Introduction

Deep Learning is a subset of machine learning. It involves neural networks that work on computational models made of multiple processing layers to learn representations of data with multiple levels of abstraction. The purpose of implementing this technology in QA is to make the QA testing approach faster and less prone to errors, which happens with the little modification in the code.

How DL Can Improve Testing of GUI

Traditional testing Methodologies involve giving a specified input checking it against the expected output and deciding the result of testing based on that. This approach of testing is susceptible to the changes made to the application and hence results in extensive automation effort. These uncertainties can be addressed by Quality risk control steps but only till a certain amount because the overall quality also becomes costly.

As part of testing methods used nowadays, tools like Selenium WebDriver break down the screen of GUI of a webpage based on the positioning, dimension, and color of elements present on the page to check that the actual output matches the desired output. If design undergoes any changes, it fails the regression for the same page, which results in significant rework, time and effort for QE to fix the code.

Under DL, we provide learning algorithms with training data to let it learned the desired functions. We also provide a set of test data and validate learning algorithms against the provided test data. This became agnostic to implementation details and less sensitive to the platforms it runs on.

The Process to Implement DL in Testing GUI

It starts with capturing the image of a webpage than divides it into various UX components, and then these components will generate the training data as well as the testing data which we feed in our model. We can now pass any newly created UX component, which gets added to the webpage to test it with the desired specification and criteria.

Test and Training Data

Test and Training Data got created by modifying the UX components of the webpage. As per design guidelines, we create our own data with respect to the input design and introduce this data as images. We label these images so that data is organized properly and then provide this data for training the model.

Modeling

This training data, along with the complexity of the scenarios which we want to cover in the testing, will decide which model(Neural Nets) we need to choose, such as SVM(Support Vector machines), CNN (Convolutional Neural Nets), or RF (Random Forests). After choosing the appropriate model, we train this model for capturing the defects in Graphical User Interface (GUI).

Advantages of DL in GUI Testing

1. This approach eliminates any deep knowledge of the domain, which makes any new intern and member in a team able to perform testing by preparing test data for a training model.

2. It makes QA testing faster as a whole team invests time to cover test coverage to feed data into the model, and not a single member requires to prepare test automation for the GUI testing.

3. Using this approach, the QA team can start their work before the development phase started using design mockups since the implementation process is irrelevant for GUI testing.

Installation of Jupyter Notebook and Kernels on Linux

The Jupyter Notebook is a web-based interactive computing environment that provides frontend access to multiple languages, and also it allows the creation of documents that contain live code and explanatory text. This section deals with the installation of the

Jupyter Notebook web application and the creation of different kernels on it.

Installation

Though Jupyter runs code in multiple programming languages, the Jupyter Notebook installation requires Python (Python 3.3 or greater, or Python 2.7). An easy way to get Jupyter is by installing the latest version of Anaconda-3, which includes over 100 built-in packages of which Jupyter Notebook is a part. As we need only Python to run Jupyter, we will go with Miniconda, which is a version of Anaconda that includes just conda, its dependencies, and Python.

Installation of Miniconda

This includes the installation of Miniconda3, which encloses Python3 and conda.

- Download Miniconda build from https://repo.continuum.io/miniconda/Miniconda3-3.19.0-Linux-x86_64.sh using wget command.

- Create a directory where Miniconda needs to be installed and run below command -

/bin/bash Miniconda3-3.19.0-Linux-x86_64.sh -f -b -p $CONDA_DIR

$CONDA_DIR is a directory where conda needs to be installed

Ex: CONDA_DIR=/usr/local

Once Miniconda is installed include Minoconda working directory in your environment variable PATH as below so that Miniconda packages can be used from any directory-

- PATH=$CONDA_DIR/bin:$PATH

Installing Jupyter on Miniconda

- As Jupyter is a conda-package, conda utility can be used to install Jupyter as below-

bash-4.1$ conda install notebook=4.2

This will download and install the dependent packages required to run Jupyter Notebook.

Once Notebook is installed it can be launched by using below command-

bash-4.1$ jupyter notebook

This launches Jupyter Notebook, which will run as a web service and can be accessed from the browser. As Jupyter is running on Python3 by default, it will have Python3 kernel on it. Each environment of conda can run only one version of Python; it can be upgraded or downgraded but cannot have multiple versions in the same environment. To get access to a different version of Python(Python2), it has been installed on different environments, and the kernel for the same needs to be created to access it from Jupyter as below.

bash-4.1$ conda create --name python2 python=2.7

bash-4.1$ source activate python2

(python2) bash-4.2$ conda install ipykernel

(python2) bash-4.2$ python -m ipykernel install

Installing BASH Kernel on Jupyter

- Install bash kernel using **pip** as below

  (jupyter)bash-4.1$ pip install bash_kernel

  (jupyter)bash-4.1$ python -m bash_kernel install

- Once the kernel is installed, launch notebook from which BASH terminal can be accessed-

Installing R Kernel on Jupyter

- Once Jupyter notebook is installed, activate the environment which has notebook package and install the kernel on it as below-

(jupyter)bash-4.1$ conda install -c r ipython-notebook r-irkernel

This will install all the dependencies required to run R on jupyter

- After installing R kernel, launch Jupyter notebook from where R can be accessed through the jupyter browser window.

- Different versions of R cannot be installed on Jupyter, but different versions of R running on the system can be made available for Jupyter by installing 'repr,' 'pbdZMQ' and 'devtools' packages on all versions of R(Note: These packages are available only on R>=3.0.2) as below.

Run the below commands on R console to install the packages-

install.packages(c('repr', 'pbdZMQ', 'devtools')) on CRAN

devtools::install_github('IRkernel/IRdisplay')

devtools::install_github('IRkernel/IRkernel')

IRkernel::installspec()

IRkernel::installspec() by default will install a kernel with the name "ir," and a display name of "R." Multiple kernels versions of R can be installed by supplying a name and display name argument to the installspec() as below.

IRkernel::installspec(name = 'ir31', displayname = 'R 3.1')   #For R 3.1

IRkernel::installspec(name = 'ir32', displayname = 'R 3.2')   #For R 3.2:

Chapter 2

Neural Networks

Introduction

Artificial Neural Networks are nothing but processing information like a Biological nervous system such as Brain, which processes information of its own. The Neural Network is composed of many interconnected elements that process information and will work in parallel to solve the specific problem. Neural Networks learn by example. Neural Networks will try to solve a problem by itself. So it does not need any other program to solve a task.

Why Neural Networks?

You may think that today's computing is very advanced to process information, then why we are going to Neural Networks. Although computing today is advanced, the computer could not process information of its own until and unless it is provided with proper information. As we know that the computer will use the Algorithm (i.e., a set of instructions) to perform a task.

A computer cannot find or solve the problem of its own. This, in turn, restricts the problem-solving capacity of the computer to perform the task that we already know. Neural Networks are very useful in this situation because we can get processed information about the problems that we don't know.

Biological Neurons

Biological neurons are made up of Cell bodies, Axon, and Dendrites. The cell body is the heart of the Cell. You may wonder how the human brain works. In the human brain, neurons receive a signal through Dendrites. And it will send the electrical activity through the long line called Axon. Axon splits into thousands of branches. At the end of each branch, there is a structure called a synapse, which is the point of contact between an axon of one cell and dendrites of another cell. Synapse converts the activity from the Axon into Electrical activity to the connected neuron. The neuron will send the narrow electrical activity down the axon. Thus the human brains learn by changing the synapses.

Simple Artificial Neural Network

The Artificial Neural Network consists of several processing elements called "NEURONS." Neurons may have many inputs but will have a single output. The output will be a numerical result. The neurons will take input from other neurons and combine them into a single output. In the below figure, X1, X2.., Xn represent inputs to the neurons.

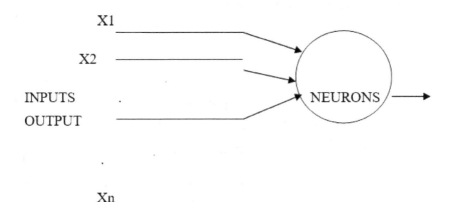

A SIMPLE NEURON

Learning Paradigm in Neural Networks

There are two types of leaning paradigm in Neural Networks; they have supervised learning and unsupervised learning.

Supervised learning: In supervised learning, the network is provided with both input and output. The network will process the input to give the desired output. The network will compare the output with the desired output.

Unsupervised learning: In unsupervised learning, the network will be provided with input only, not the desired output. The network, by itself, processes the information to give the output. It is referred to as Self-Organization.

Application of Neural Networks

Some of the real-time applications of Neural Networks are as follows,

1. Instant doctor - The network is trained to store a large number of medical records, includes symptoms, diagnosis, and treatment for a particular disease.

2. Security -It will identify the person by our fingerprint itself. This will help in not carrying bunches of keys.

3. Military - The network is trained to differentiate between the rocks and mines.

4. Stock Market Prediction – Neural Networks is trained to predict the stock prices based upon the result in the past.

Pattern Recognition

Pattern recognition is one of the applications of Neural Networks. Pattern recognition is used to differentiate between two objects by using their shape, texture, and weight. For example, assume that in a fruit warehouse where we store different fruits when the fruits are brought to the warehouse, they may get mixed and so we need to store them separately. Using the Sorter machine, we can sort out the fruits.

Here, for example, we will take two fruits, apple, and orange.

In a sorter machine, we have a conveyer belt where the fruits are loaded. The conveyer belt will pass through the SENSOR where 3 Parameter such as Shape, Texture, and Weight is measured. For approximately round shape, the Sensor will give 1 else -1. If the texture is smooth, the sensor will give 1 else -1. If the weight of the fruit is more than a pound, then the sensor will give 1 else -1. Depending upon the result from the sensor, the sorter will sort the fruits and store it in the respective bins.

The vector representation will be p = (Shape, Texture, and Weight)

Apple   = (-1, 1, -1)

Orange   = (1, -1, 1)

Simple Pattern Recognition Using Neural Network

This chapter focuses on identifying simple patterns which it learns through training. In our daily life, we got several texts where pixels are not properly printed. Sometimes some extra pixels come, or some pixels got deleted. But our brain read it properly from previous learning. Same thing I have implemented here to recognize simple patterns like addition (+), Subtraction (-), Multiplication (X), etc. Here we will use the Hopfield neural network to recognize the pattern.

Terminology

Before starting, I would like to introduce some terminologies which are going to be used:

Neural processing: How do we recognize a face in a crowd? When we see a face, the basic unit of our brain (neuron) starts working on that information asynchronously and finally gives the result as an output. This biological processing is called neural processing, and it inspires us for artificial neural processing.

Neural network: This is a computational structure where each processing unit works asynchronously and is assumed to have functional behavior in the same manner as our neuron.

Weight: This is the number or value given on the edges connecting different layers of neurons. These values have a significant role in neural processing.

Actions on Neurons

According to the weight of neurons, there are two possible actions on it:

1. Start with a weight matrix and remain the same throughout the execution, i.e., no external training is required.

2. Start with a weight matrix, and some or all weight of the matrix changes during execution, i.e., it requires external training.

Neural Network Construction

There are three aspects of neural network construction:

- Structure: This relates how many layers the network should contain, what their functions are, and input-output.

- Encoding: This changes the weight matrix during execution.

- Recall: This relates to the recall of the previous result.

Description

Any letter or picture can be shown as a sequence of pixels. Suppose we want to show summation (+) sign in 3 X 3 pixel matrix then it will be looking like:

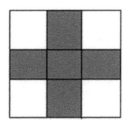

Now we can give the pattern of this sign in binary form as (0, 1, 0, 1, 1, 1, 0, 1, 0). Here every white pixel value is zero, and the blue pixel is one. Now if we replace 0 with -1 then the vector which we get bipolar vector as (-1, 1, -1, 1, 1, 1, -1, 1, -1). Similarly for minus sign we will get (-1, -1, -1, 1, 1, 1, -1, -1, -1).

Now we will give an input pattern, and the network will try to recognize it according to training. To recognize a pattern, the given input vector is multiplied by the **Weight Matrix**: The elements of the resultant vector are compared to a threshold function and return 1 or -1. Now the value got after comparison forms a bipolar vector. Here the function is –

f(x) = 1 if x>= threshold Value

= -1 if x< threshold value.

This vector remains the same as some recognizable vector given at the time of training. Here the weight matrix is designed in such a way that it will always generate the same pattern. For example plus-minus the weight matrix is

0 0 2 -2 -2 -2 2 0 2

0 0 0 0 0 0 0 2 0

2 0 0 -2 -2 -2 2 0 2

W= -2 0 -2 0 2 2 -2 0 -2

-2 0 -2 2 0 2 -2 0 -2

-2 0 -2 2 2 0 -2 0 -2

2 0 2 -2 -2 -2 0 0 2

0 2 0 0 0 0 0 0 0

2 0 2 -2 -2 -2 2 0 0

Now suppose if we get a plus sign like

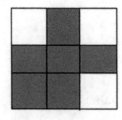

We can easily say that this is a plus sign by looking at it. Now it's corresponding bipolar vector is B(-1, 1, -1, 1, 1, 1, 1, 1, -1). If we find $B \times W$ we get a vector with values C (-40, 28, -20, 40, 0, 40, -20, 28, -40). Now we fix the threshold value at 0(zero). Then the vector that we get from threshold function is (-1, 1, -1, 1, 1, 1, -1, 1, -1). It is the same as the training vector of plus.

The weight matrix of the pattern is derived from the bipolar vector of it.

To convert any binary vector to bipolar, we use the function

f(x) = 2x-1 where x the elements of binary vector and f(x) is corresponding bipolar element. Now we transpose the vector and multiply this transposed one with original vector. Finally subtraction of 1 from diagonal elements gives the weight matrix for this pattern. For example plus (+) sign we can get the weight matrix as follows-

P = [-1, 1, -1, 1, 1, 1, -1, 1, -1]

-1

1

-1

P^T =   1

1

1

-1

1

-1

Now $P^T X P$ can be given as

-1   [-1 1 -1 1 1 1 -1 1 -1]   1 -1 1 -1 -1 -1 1 -1 1

1   -1 1 -1 1 1 1 -1 1 -1

-1   1 -1 1 -1 -1 -1 1 -1 1

       1   -1 1 -1 1 1 1 -1 1 -1

1   =   -1 1 -1 1 1 1 -1 1 -1

1   -1 1 -1 1 1 1 -1 1 -1

-1   1 -1 1 -1 -1 -1 1 -1 1

1   -1 1 -1 1 1 1 -1 1 -1

-1   1 -1 1 -1 -1 -1 1 -1 1

Now weight matrix can be given by subtracting 1 from each diagonal element. It is the same as subtracting the identity matrix. For every pattern that the network has to recognize generates weight matrix as above shown. Finally, after adding all the weight matrix generated by all the patterns, it gives the resultant weight matrix.

Application

We initially try to train the system with a base pattern by providing the pixel orientation of each pattern and a corresponding image of the pattern for visual recognition. We choose (+) (-) (X) and (/) as base symbols.

After clicking on done, we give our input as above and test it to recognize the pattern.

Here is the code for the above program.

```
using System;

using System.Collections.Generic;

using System.ComponentModel;

using System.Data;

using System.Drawing;

using System.Linq;

using System.Text;

using System.Windows.Forms;

namespace NeuralNetworkProjects

{

    public partial class PatternRecognision : Form
```

```csharp
{
    // Variable declare section.

    public static int[,] weightMatrix= new int[9, 9];

    List<PatternPicPair> givenPatterns = new
List<PatternPicPair>();

    static int[,] flag = new int[1, 9]{{-1, -1, -1, -1, -1, -1, -
1, -1, -1}};


    // This function generates weigth matrix dynamically.

    public void weightMatrixGeneration (int[,] pattern)

    {
        int[,] transpose = new int[9, 1];

        int[,] transposeMul = new int[9, 9];

        // Transposing the matrix

        for (int i = 0; i < 9; i++)

        {
            transpose[i, 0] = pattern[0, i];

        }
```

```
        transposeMul = matrixMull(transpose, pattern, 9, 1,
1, 9);

        for (int i = 0; i < 9; i++)

            for (int j = 0; j < 9; j++)

                weightMatrix[i, j] = weightMatrix[i, j] +
transposeMul[i, j]; // Final weight matix generation after
addition.

    }

    public PatternRecognision()

    {

        InitializeComponent();

    }


    private void button1_Click(object sender, EventArgs e)

    {

        int[,] toCheck = new int[1, 9];

        int[,] finResul = new int[1, 9];
```

```
toCheck = matrixMull(flag, weightMatrix, 1, 9, 9,
9); // Multiplying given input pattern weight weigth matrix.
It will generate a 1x9 matrix.

bool[] flgRecog = new bool[givenPatterns.Count];

// Getting values after comparing with threshold
value.

for (int ix = 0; ix < 9; ix++)

{

    if (toCheck[0, ix] >= 0)

        finResul[0, ix] = 1;

    else

        finResul[0, ix] = -1;

}

//Making decision for that pattern

for(int i = 0; i < givenPatterns.Count; i++)

{

    for( int j = 0; j < 9; j++)

    {
```

```
                if(givenPatterns[i].Pattern[0, j] == finResul[0,
j])

                    flgRecog[i] = true;

                else

                {

                    flgRecog[i] = false;

                    break;

                }

            }

        }

        {

            bool flgUndefined = true;

            // Showing the pattern as result

            for (int i = 0; i < givenPatterns.Count; i++)

            {

                if (flgRecog[i] == true)

                {

                    flgUndefined = false;
```

```
                pbResult.ImageLocation =
givenPatterns[i].FilePath;

                    flgRecog[i] = false;

            }

        }

        if(flgUndefined == true)

            pbResult.ImageLocation =
"D:\\Examples\\Undetermined.png";



    }

}


    // This function will give a matrix which is the
multiplication of two matrix

    public int[,] matrixMull( int[,] first, int[,]second, int
firstRowCount, int firstColumnCount, int secondRowCount,
int secondColumnCount )

    {

        int [,]returnValue = new int[firstRowCount,
secondColumnCount];
```

```csharp
        for (int i = 0; i < firstRowCount; i++)

            for (int j = 0; j < firstColumnCount; j++)

                for (int k = 0; k < secondColumnCount; k++)

                    returnValue[i, k] += first[i, j] * second[j, k];

            return returnValue;

        }

        #region input image setting

        private void pictureBox1_Click(object sender,
EventArgs e)

        {

            if (flag[0, 0] == -1)

            {

                flag[0, 0] = 1;

                pictureBox1.ImageLocation =
"D:\\Examples\\black.png";

            }

            else

            {
```

```csharp
            flag[0, 0] = -1;

            pictureBox1.ImageLocation =
"D:\\Examples\\white.png";

        }

    }


    private void pictureBox2_Click(object sender,
EventArgs e)

    {

        if (flag[0, 1] == -1)

        {

            flag[0, 1] = 1;

            pictureBox2.ImageLocation =
"D:\\Examplesblack.png";

        }

        else

        {

            flag[0, 1] = -1;
```

```csharp
            pictureBox2.ImageLocation =
"D:\\Examples\\white.png";

        }

    }

    private void pictureBox3_Click(object sender,
EventArgs e)

    {

        if (flag[0, 2] == -1)

        {

            flag[0, 2] = 1;

            pictureBox3.ImageLocation =
"D:\\Examples\\black.png";

        }

        else

        {

            flag[0, 2] = -1;

            pictureBox3.ImageLocation =
"D:\\Examples\\white.png";

        }
```

```csharp
        }

        private void pictureBox4_Click(object sender,
EventArgs e)

        {

            if (flag[0, 3] == -1)

            {

                flag[0, 3] = 1;

                pictureBox4.ImageLocation =
"D:\\Examples\\black.png";

            }

            else

            {

                flag[0, 3] = -1;

                pictureBox4.ImageLocation =
"D:\\Examples\\white.png";

            }

        }

        private void pictureBox5_Click(object sender,
EventArgs e)
```

```
        {

            if (flag[0, 4] == -1)

            {

                flag[0, 4] = 1;

                pictureBox5.ImageLocation =
"D:\\Examples\\black.png";

            }

            else

            {

                flag[0, 4] = -1;

                pictureBox5.ImageLocation =
"D:\\Examples\\white.png";

            }

        }

        private void pictureBox6_Click(object sender,
EventArgs e)

        {

            if (flag[0, 5] == -1)
```

```
        {

            flag[0, 5] = 1;

            pictureBox6.ImageLocation =
"D:\\Examples\\black.png";

        }

        else

        {

            flag[0, 5] = -1;

            pictureBox6.ImageLocation =
"D:\\Examples\\white.png";

        }

    }

    private void pictureBox7_Click(object sender,
EventArgs e)

    {

        if (flag[0, 6] == -1)

        {

            flag[0, 6] = 1;
```

```csharp
            pictureBox7.ImageLocation =
"D:\\Examples\\black.png";

        }

        else

        {

            flag[0, 6] = -1;

            pictureBox7.ImageLocation =
"D:\\Examples\\white.png";

        }

    }

    private void pictureBox8_Click(object sender,
EventArgs e)

    {

        if (flag[0, 7] == -1)

        {

            flag[0, 7] = 1;

            pictureBox8.ImageLocation =
"D:\\Examples\\black.png";

        }
```

```
else

{

    flag[0, 7] = -1;

    pictureBox8.ImageLocation =
"D:\\Examples\\white.png";

    }

}

private void pictureBox9_Click(object sender,
EventArgs e)

{

    if (flag[0, 8] == -1)

    {

        flag[0, 8] = 1;

        pictureBox9.ImageLocation =
"D:\\Examples\\black.png";

    }

    else

    {
```

```
        flag[0, 8] = -1;

        pictureBox9.ImageLocation =
"D:\\Examples\\white.png";

    }

}

#endregion

// This function calls another function to generate
weight matrix dynamically for every input pattern.

    private void btnTrain_Click(object sender, EventArgs
e)

    {

        for (int i = 0; i < givenPatterns.Count; i++)

            weightMatrixGeneration(givenPatterns[i].Pattern);

    }

// This function is used to set initial pattern based on which
we have to recognize another pattern

    private void btnAddPattern_Click(object sender,
EventArgs e)

    {
```

```
bool blnkFlag = true;

// Checking for blank input.

for (int i = 0; i < 9; i++)

{

    if (flag[0, i] == 1)

    {

        blnkFlag = false;

        break;

    }

    else

        blnkFlag = true;

}

    if (blnkFlag == true)

    MessageBox.Show("Please provide a pattern");

else

{

        // Getting the pattern as well as corresponding
image
```

```csharp
MessageBox.Show("Please select a picture corresponding to this pattern");

openFileDialog1.ShowDialog();

string strFilePath = openFileDialog1.FileName;

PatternPicPair objPatternPic = new PatternPicPair();

objPatternPic.FilePath = strFilePath;

int[,] pattern = new int[1, 9];

for (int i = 0; i < 9; i++)

    objPatternPic.Pattern[0, i] = flag[0, i];;

givenPatterns.Add(objPatternPic);

for (int i = 0; i < 9; i++)

{

    flag[0, i] = -1;

}

// Here we set all the input pixel to initial form.

pictureBox1.ImageLocation = "D:\\Examples\\white.png";
```

```
        pictureBox2.ImageLocation =
"D:\\Examples\\white.png";

        pictureBox3.ImageLocation =
"D:\\Examples\\white.png";

        pictureBox4.ImageLocation =
"D:\\Examples\\white.png";

        pictureBox5.ImageLocation =
"D:\\Examples\\white.png";

        pictureBox6.ImageLocation =
"D:\\Examples\\white.png";

        pictureBox7.ImageLocation =
"D:\\Examples\\white.png";

        pictureBox8.ImageLocation =
"D:\\Examples\\white.png";

        pictureBox9.ImageLocation =
"D:\\Examples\\white.png";

        }

    }
```

// This function stops further input of any pattern and show the train and recognize button.

```csharp
        private void btnDone_Click(object sender, EventArgs
e)

    {

        btnAddPattern.Visible = false;

        btnDone.Visible = false;

        btnTrain.Visible = true;

        btnRecognize.Visible = true;

    }

}

// This class create the structure of a pattern as well as
take the path of the picture corresponding the that picture.

public class PatternPicPair{

    int[,] pattern = new int[1, 9];

    public int[,] Pattern

    {

        get { return pattern; }

        set { pattern = value; }

    }
```

```
string filePath = "";

public string FilePath

{

    get { return filePath; }

    set { filePath = value; }

}

}

}
```

Conclusion

1. When a pattern is contained by another pattern like division (\) and multiplication where division (\) is contained by multiplication (X), then it will give the superset pattern. This is happening even a pixel is not present.

We can see that 3, 1 pixel is blank, but the program will recognize it at a multiplication, not as division because here division is contained by multiplication.

Similarly, it will recognize the above two pictures as plus not minus.

2. When a pattern is a merge of two patterns where one pattern is not a subset of another pattern, and the number of pixels is the same, then it will not be able to recognize the pattern. For example:

We can see the pattern contains two patterns a minus as well as a division (both containing three pixels), but no one is the subset of another one, so the program is not able to recognize this pattern.

3. When a pattern is the merge of two known patterns, and no one is a subset of another one, then it will recognize the pattern which has a higher pixel number.

Here the first pattern will be recognized as multiplication (X), not minus (-). Similarly, the second pattern will be recognized as plus (+), not division (\) as the weight of multiplication(X) in the first case and plus (+) in the second case.

Artificial Neural Network

We all have a basic idea of what a neural network is. Based on the neural network theory only, a human's brain is functioning. This theory clearly explains how the neurons in the brain work and how it is providing information and efforts for the creation of artificial intelligence. A neural network (also known as Biological Neural network) is the composition of a bunch of neurons. A single neuron is connected with the other neurons present in the brain. Basically, these neurons are formed with axons and dendrites. These neurons are connected within the peripheral nervous system / Central nervous system.

What is Artificial Neural Network (ANN)?

Artificial Neural network is developed based on the structure of a brain. The functionality of an ANN is also similar to a brain. The network is made of a large number of highly interconnected elements (otherwise called neurons). These interconnected neurons work in parallel to get a solution for a specific problem. Also, it can analyze and recognize patterns, able to manage any data, and learn easily. Neural networks learn by example. This ANN is completely composed of artificial neurons and implements the essence of a biological neuron.

An artificial neuron was developed by the neurophysiologist Warren McCulloch and the logician Walter pits during 1943 for the first time. As the technologies available were very less in that period, they were not able to proceed with this in detail.

Artificial networks placed its footprints not only in Sales forecasting, Industrial Process Control, Data validation, Risk management, Customer research, and marketing but also in the medical field. An artificial neural network is playing a very important role in medical science. Advanced features such as computers, Ultrasonic imaging, lasers, and many more are helping/boosting medicine to improve its level of achievement.

Artificial Neural Networks in Medicine
Artificial neural networks could be used in every situation in which exists a relationship between some variables that can be considered inputs and other variables that can be predicted. Artificial Neural network is an important research area in the medical field nowadays. Using an artificial neural network, it can be monitored a lot of health indices such as blood pressure, glucose level, respiration rate, etc. or can be predicted the patient's response to therapy. Using Scans, the neural network can easily recognize any

disease. Hence there is no need to write any specific algorithm about the details of identifying a disease. This has been successfully applied in a few areas such as Drug development, Bio-medical analysis, Image analysis, etc.

In diagnostic systems, there is a wide usage of ANN's. In this kind of process, ANN's are used to analyze heart and cancer problems.

In Image analysis, artificial neural networks are used to detect tumors in ultra-sonograms, MRI (Magnetic Resonance Images) scanning for the classification of vessel and tissue classification, x-ray classifications, and also the determination of skeletal image through x-ray images.

In Drug development, artificial neural networks are used for the development of drugs and medicines for the treatment of cancer and AIDS.

In the biochemical analysis, artificial neural networks are used to analyze blood and urine samples; also, it helps to detect the pathological conditions such as Tuberculosis, helps to track the level of glucose in diabetics.

Diagnosis and Modeling of Cardio System

To model the cardiovascular system in human beings, Neural Network is being used extensively with the help of Deep Learning. The initial diagnosis is performed by model preparation of an individual's cardiovascular system and then comparing the model with the actual physiological values of the patient. By regularly following the mechanism under a supervised and well-disciplined process, then life-threatening medical conditions will get detected at an early stage itself, and the patient's life can be saved. The modeling of the cardio system should impersonate the relationship between the variables found at various levels.

The variables consist of blood pressure, heartbeat, breathing rate, and other relevant tests. The personalized model created with the help of Deep Learning will only be used for a single person and will not be applicable to other patients. This is necessary because each patient is different and should be treated accordingly. The automatic simulation must have the ability to adjust the features without taking help from a supervisor. Therefore, the Neural Network comes into play.

Artificial Neural Network is capable of providing sensor fusion technology, which will combine different sensor values and then detect the serious medical conditions with the infusion of data from other biomedical sensor devices. Due to this technology, it is now possible to detect life-threatening medical conditions like heart attacks and cancer very quickly. The doctor will be able to make the decisions quickly and efficiently.

Pattern Recognition of Pathology Images

Pathology is an imaging technique in medicine which deals with the nature of the disease, could be functional, or any structural changes in the tissues in our body. As it needs perfect color and high resolution makes the use of digital image technology, and it is very difficult to implement. Pattern Recognition – It is an idea of dividing the input data into certain individual classes by the use of significant feature attributes of the data.

The features of a neural network like Deep Learning and Machine learning are used extensively in pattern recognition. With the parallel nature that the artificial neural network has, it can achieve a very high computation rate, which is vital in many medical applications.

Advantages of Artificial Neural Network

1. When an element of the neural network fails, it can continue without any problem by their parallel nature.

2. A neural network learns, hence does not need to be reprogrammed.

3. It can be implemented in any application without any problem.

Disadvantages of Artificial Neural Network

1. Neural networks need the training to operate.

2. It requires high processing time for large neural networks.

The architecture of a neural network is different from the architecture of microprocessors. Hence it needs to be emulated.

Chapter 3

Speech Recognition
Using Deep Learning

Introduction

Speech recognition, in other words, is the inter-disciplinary sub-field or a sub-part of computational linguistics. This field develops technologies and methodologies that help in translation and recognition of the language spoken into text by computers. It is also known as "computer speech recognition," automatic speech recognition, or "speech to text." It incorporates research and knowledge in linguistics, electrical engineering, and computer science fields.

What are Speaker Dependent Systems?

Some of the Speech recognition systems use enrolment or training in which the speaker reads out a text or sentences into the system. The system analyses the speaker's voice, pronunciation, etc. to optimize the recognition of the person's speech. This increases accuracy drastically. These types of systems are known as Speaker dependent systems. Similarly, the systems which do not use this enrolment or training process are known as speaker-independent systems.

Application of Speech Recognition

Applications of Speech Recognition include "voice user interfaces" such as:

- Call routing
- Voice dialing
- Robotic appliance control
- Simple data entry
- Search
- Preparation of structured documents
- Direct Voice Input in aircrafts
- Speech to text processing

Note: The term "Speaker Identification" or "Voice recognition" refers to the identification of the speaker's voice only. This process can help in simplification of the "speech translation to text" task. It is also used in authentication and verification of the speaker's identity; thus, enhancing the security.

The speech recognition technology had largely benefitted because of advancements in the fields of big data and deep learning.

Methods, Models, and Algorithms

Hidden Markov Models

In modern times, the speech recognition systems make use of the Hidden Markov Models. In this type of model, a speech signal is seen as a short time piecewise stationary signal. Besides this, there are many useful properties of this model, such as simplicity, easy automatic training, and computational feasibility.

Dynamic Time Warping (DTW)-Based Speech Recognition

Before being replaced by the HMM-based approach, the Dynamic time warping approach was used in speech recognition. In this type of algorithm, similarities are measured in-between two sequences that can vary in speed or time.

Neural Networks

In the late 1980s, neural networks became a very attractive approach to acoustic modeling. It has been used in various aspects of speech recognition, namely speaker adaptation, audiovisual speaker recognition, and audiovisual speech recognition.

Unlike HMMs, no assumptions are made about the statistical properties of neural networks. Besides this, the neural network has many other useful qualities and features which make it an attractive model. When it is used for the estimation of the speech feature segment's probabilities, discriminative training efficiently and naturally is allowed by the neural networks. Neural networks make few assumptions on the Input feature statistics. Neural networks are not too much success for recognition tasks that are continuous because of its diminished ability to modeling temporal dependencies. It is effective in the classification of short term units such as isolated words and individual phones.

In recent times TDNN or Time Delay Neural Networks and LSTM RNN OR Recurrent Neural Networks are being used, which can identify temporal dependencies that are latent. By using this information, the task of speech recognition is performed.

Deep Neural Networks are being researched and experimented with to effectively tackle this problem.

Due to the diminished ability of neural networks for modeling temporal dependencies, a different and alternative approach is being tested to use neural networks as pre-processing. For example, dimensionality reduction, transformation for HMM-based recognition.

MFCC Algorithm

MFCC uses voice samples as input values. Unique Coefficients are calculated after processing for a sample. The easy implementation makes MFCC the most preferred technique in voice recognition.

Generation of Coefficients

Speech Signal y(n) sent to high pass filter:

$$o(n) = y(n) - a * y(n - 1)$$

o(n) is the output signal with value between 0.9 and 1.0 usually.

The Z transform is:

$$H(z) = 1 - a * z^{-1}$$

The other process includes Frame Blocking, Hamming Window, Fast Fourier Transform, Triangular Bandpass Filters, and Discrete Fourier transform.

The input speech signal is first made continuous. For facilitating the Fast Fourier transform, the frame size or sample points is taken such that it is equal to the power of two. If the criteria are not fulfilled, then conduction of zero paddings is done to fulfill the criteria. Sometimes overlapping is used to produce continuity in frames. This is known as Frame blocking.

For continuity of the starting and ending points of the frame, a frame is multiplied with a hamming window. After this process, the Fast Fourier Transform is done. It is for checking the magnitude frequency response. For conducting FFT, the signal should be continuous and periodic. So the non-continuous or non-periodic signals are multiplied with the Hamming window to get desired results.

After this process, the result (magnitude frequency response) is multiplied with a 40-triangular set bandpass filter. It is done to know log energy for every Triangular bandpass filter. And lastly, to get the L Mel cepstral coefficients, DFT or Discrete Fourier Transform is applied to the output.

Implementation

Voice Recognition is widely used nowadays. It has made work a lot easier for users. Some of the applications that make use of this technology are as follows:

- Microsoft Cortana
- Google Assistant
- Dragon
- Indigo
- CMU Sphinx
- HTK
- Mozilla Deep Speech
- Julius
- Iatros
- Kaldi
- Agnitio
- RWTH ASR

Besides these, there are numerous other speech recognition applications.

Nowadays, artificial intelligence is also being implemented to these applications, which are enhancing the usability and interactive capability of these applications to a large extent.

The applications are acting as virtual assistants that interact with the user and carry out various tasks such as playing music, searching, having a conversation, opening a secondary application, reading out stories, and much more.

Advantages and Disadvantages

Advantages

1. It is very useful for people who are visually impaired.

2. People with physical problems make typing difficult for them to benefit a lot from this.

3. It helps in making the authentication process more secure, for example, unlocking a system with voice.

4. Saves a lot of time by carrying out activities easily and instantly without the need of tedious typing.

5. Typing a narration for the user. The user will just have to read out, and the software will do the typing process.

Disadvantages

1. Misinterpretation and lack of accuracy: Speech recognition software does not always identify words correctly every time. It is because it cannot understand the context like humans. It also faces a problem with homonyms such as "there" and "their." Also, it might face problems with acronyms, technical words, and slangs.

2. Accents: People have different accents, and they pronounce the words differently. Speech recognition software has

problems coping up with the accents. Though some of the applications are made to learn over time, still initial errors are observed. Also, the user has to speak consistently. Going too fast or slow might lead to errors. Change in voice due to sore throat or cold might also lead to errors.

3. Time Costs and Productivity: Finding the right tone and pace takes time. Though some of the applications learn the accent and pace nowadays, still it takes time for it to reduce the errors and work correctly. Adaptation takes time, and a lot of effort of the user is spent in getting punctuation right and learning system commands.

4. Background Noise Interference: A quiet environment is needed for getting the optimal performance of the speech recognition software. Background noise can lead to errors and misinterpretations. Users can reduce it by using high-quality microphones.

5. Physical Side Effects: Vocal problems and physical discomfort are observed among users. Usage of voice recognition software for extended periods can lead to muscle fatigue, dry mouth, hoarseness, vocal strain, and temporary loss of voice. Talking unnaturally can make the situation worse.

Sentence Generation Using NLG

Natural language processing has been a point of interest since the 1950s when Alan Turing proposed a criterion for intelligence known as "Turing Test." NLP deals with human-computer interaction which focusses on computers able to derive meaning from human (natural) language. It finds its applications in various fields like Machine translation, fighting spam, extracting information, summarization, answering queries, etc. One very significant application of NLP is artificial intelligence which is the emerging field of research and development. Natural Language generation comprises of three major aspects, namely: Syntax, Semantics, and Pragmatics. Syntax refers to the grammar of the language, and semantics refers to the meaning while pragmatics component deals with how it is related to the world.

Natural language generation, on the other hand, deals with generating human language from computer representation of logical form or any knowledge base. It finds its applications in generating textual summaries, weather forecasting, etc.

In this section, we all learn how to process a given set of words and generate a simple sentence using them.

Parts of Speech Tagging (POST)

Also known as word-category disambiguation, which deals with identifying a word in a sentence as a particular part of speech. It is a part of Natural language processing.

To generate a sentence from a given set of legitimate words, we need to identify them as different parts of speech first.

E.g., In the given sentence, if we do a POST

And now for something completely different

And: Coordinating conjunction

Now: Adverb

For: Preposition / subordinating conjunction

Something: Noun

Completely: Adverb

Different: Adjective

There are many APIs for NLP. The API in java that we used for implementing the same is edu.standford.nlp. By using this API, we can build a system that can take a set of words as input as mark them as different parts of speech. We can then generate a sentence using identified parts of speech.

The API has classes like CoreLabel, TokenizerFactory, lexicalizedParser, CorelabeltokenFactory, PTBTokenizer, Tokenizer, Tree, and many more, which enable us to build a POST module.

We first initialize a parser and parse each word generating a tree in which parent node is an identifying label and leaf node is the word. We can then traverse the tree to find out which word belongs to which part of speech and generate the sentence.

Sentence Generation

Let's take a set of words with which we want to generate a sentence

(Mary, chase, cat)

In the sentence which we want to form, let's identify the tokens as different parts of speech

Mary is the subject,

Chase the verb and

Cat the object.

By using a natural language generation system, we can then generate a sentence as "Mary chases the cat."

The Java API used for the same is the simple Nlg, which has various classes like Lexicon, Framework, Features, Realizer, Phrasespec, which enable us to build a system that can generate sentences from identified parts of speech.

After importing the required packages and classes we can create a simple sentence as:

Lexicon lexicon = Lexicon.getDefaultLexicon();

    NLGFactory nlgFactory = new NLGFactory(lexicon);

    Realiser realiser = new Realiser(lexicon);

    SPhraseSpec p = nlgFactory.createClause();

```
p.setSubject("Mary");

p.setVerb("chase");

p.setObject("the cat");

String sentence = realiser.realiseSentence(p);
```

We can also set the tense of the sentence as:

```
p.setFeature(Feature.TENSE, Tense.PRESENT);
```

We can also add complements, adjectives, and prepositions and generate sentences using multiple subjects and objects.

As an example, we input the name of a java function calculateInterest(int principal, int rate, int time) to the designed system and got a summary of its functionality in the form of a sentence from its tokens to calculate, interest, principal, rate, time.

Such are the wonders and power of NLP and NLG.

We have so many useful classes in NLP and NLG APIs for java, which we can use for processing and analyzing sentences as well as generating new sentences. The potential application lies in analyzing a piece of technical or non- technical code and generating its summary.

Chapter 4

Word Embedding in Python and Linear Regression Modeling

NLP-Word Embedding In Python

Natural language processing (NLP) deals with building computational algorithms that can automatically understand, analyze, and represent human language. Systems which are NLP based, have enabled applications such as Google's powerful search engine, amazon Alexa, etc. With a spike in the usability of NLP algorithms and the generation of more data from various sources, the techniques to deal with natural language is evolving every day. This paper gives a surface level explanation of one of the widely used techniques known as word embedding in NLP space.

Natural Language Processing is the technology and also called machine learning. The process of Converting or extracting human language to meaningful machine language.

NLP is used to analyze text, allowing the machine to understand how humans speak. Commonly used for text mining (is the process of deriving high-quality information from the text), machine translation, and automated question answering.

Why NLP?

Natural language processing is mainly used for Information Extraction and Machine Translation

1. Information Extraction

Information extraction is the process of NLP used to extract Structured or detailed information in a simplified way.

Example:

- We planned for the outing tomorrow at 6:00 pm in the Phoenix Mall, Los Angeles

To do: Outing

Time: 05:00 pm, 21/12/2019

Venue: Phoenix Mall, Los Angeles

Below topics are the other important applications of Natural Language Processing.

2. Text Summarization

Getting Keywords for the large text or like an acronym. To create an abstract of a well-designed article.

3. Context Analysis

The technique in NLP is basically used to analyzing a simple text and extract the context of the text or sentence.

4. Sentiment Analysis

It is done with the help of Natural Language Processing to identify, quantify, study, and extract the various subjective information. It is mainly used for knowing the customer reviews and their opinions regarding your products and services. They cover social media posts, marketing, emails, telephonic calls, and chats.

Example:

> Service about the Hotels:
>
> Best roast chicken in New York."
>
> "Service was very nice."
>
> Another set of reviews
>
> "iPhone 11 is over-hyped."
>
> "The hype about iPhone 11 is justified."

Tasks in NLP

- Contextual analysis
- Sentiment analysis
- Text/Sentence Classification
- Modeling the Language

Segmentation

It is the process of segmenting text into words by writing it into meaningful sentences and topics. It is a combination of the brain used by humans and the AI processes used in network systems. The main delimiter used in the languages is the spacebar.

"The meeting has been scheduled for this Sunday,"

"He has agreed to co-operate with me."

"Indigo Airlines introduces another flight on the Dubai - Singapore route.'

"We are leaving for Washington on 26th June."

Modeling the Language

This technique in NLP is the subtask, and simple task compare to another task in NLP and it is used for spelling correction, recognition of handwriting, and meaningful machine translation.

To create headlines for newly created articles.

To create new documents and sentences.

POS Tagging

Part of Speech (POS) recognition

"Mary speaks good English."

Mary	Speaks	Good	English
Noun	Verb	adjective	Noun

Word Sense Disambiguation (WSD)

In Natural Language Processing Technique word sensing nothing but identifying which meaning is used in the sentence, when the word has multiple meanings.

For example, there are two sentences in the paragraph; particular words used in the sentences are the same but different meanings.

What is Word Embedding?

Word embedding is a type of word representation where a word is represented as a dense vector (a vector with most entries as non-zero), which captures details about the meaning of the word.

The purpose of doing this is, different words with similar meanings have a similar vector representation.

Understanding Word Embedding

Let us take a sentence for demo purpose – **"A monkey was jumping on my table with coconut in hands nearby my wardrobe."**

After basic processing of the above sentence, when it goes through a word embedding algorithm, then words in the sentence will be given a vector representation based on its features. Let us take four words for our example.

Monkey, Table, Coconut, Wardrobe

Let us assume 3 features for better understanding

Is_wood

Is_animal

Is_black

Now, all of the above words will be given a score between 0 to 1(a simple approach, for example) on the above-listed features. A sample table could look like below table

	Monkey	Table	Coconut	Wardrobe
Is_wood	0.01	0.95	0.03	0.95
Is_Black	0.5	0.8	0.6	0.92
Is_animal	0.98	0.05	0.02	0.03

The above table is nothing but a vector representation of given words.

For example, Monkey is (0.01, 0.5, and 0.98) and Coconut is (0.03, 0.6, and 0.02)

If we embed these vectors in a (3 in this case) dimensional space, then the process is called word embedding, and words with similar meaning will appear to be closer in the space. (Distance wise).

A two dimensional PCA decomposed feature vectors looked like below in python plot

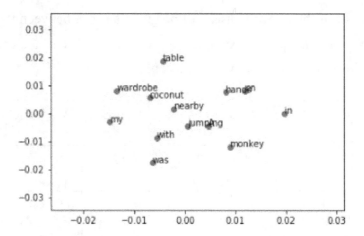

Image Source – This is plotted on my desktop python using personal data

As expected, the monkey is far from the table and wardrobe, and the coconut is far from the table, whereas the table and wardrobe seem to be closer.

Ways to Use the Word Embedding Model

There are two ways we can do word embedding in Python.

1. Train our model of word embedding and use it

2. Use a pre-trained model

Generally, for training a word embedding model in python, a genism package is used. Process wise it looks simple to train a model, however for a good model lot of preprocessing and domain-specific knowledge is needed otherwise performance-wise, it might not be great. This approach also needs a huge amount of text, like millions or billions of words for useful learning.

Python code to train the model.

I am giving my word tokenized sentence input here.

let us define the training data first

my_sentence = [['A', 'monkey', 'was', 'jumping', 'on', 'my', 'table', 'with', 'coconut', 'in', 'hands', 'nearby', 'my', 'wardrobe']]

train model

model = Word2Vec(sentences, min_count = 1)

Get most similar word to table

model.wv.most_similar("table")

As per output, there is a score generated for each word in sentence on "how similar they are to word "table""

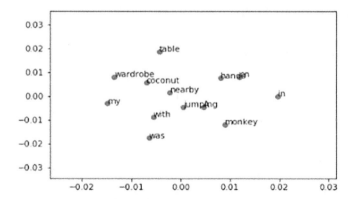

"Wardrobe" is closest as expected.

Word2Vec and Glove

As discussed above, training the own word embedding model need a huge corpus, domain expertise, and a lot of disc space. An alternative is to use pre-trained models available.

Word2vec

This pre-trained model contains tokens as well as word vectors in it. The size of the file is approximately 1.5 GB. It is made available by Google for general purpose usage.

Once downloaded, the model can be used directly.

Glove

Similar to Google's Word2vec, researchers from Stanford found their own algorithm for word embedding named GloVe.

Download link for the same is:

http://nlp.stanford.edu/data/glove.6B.zip

Different versions/types of GloVe are available at below GitHub location:

https://github.com/stanfordnlp/GloVe

A glove model can be used in two steps.

1. First, convert the downloaded file to Word2Vec.

2. Next, use this converted file as we did in Word2Vec.

Therefore basics of word embedding and its implementation in python are covered. There are a lot of other techniques that can be used for feature extraction from the text.

Linear Regression Using Python

Today technology is growing at a strong pace, and so are the tools and methods to shape it. Now booking tickets, may it be of movies, airplanes, shows or any other deal is just two minutes job with technology advancements. So moving with the belief that technology is still impacting us is a good side to move with.

One such technology is Machine learning. Machine learning is an aspect of AI where a machine is trained on data to perform its functions. It mainly analyzes input data so to performs pattern calculation on it and predict the required features.

Traditionally machines were loaded with predefined procedures that used to be performed on input data, and that was their only job. But with advancements, these procedures became more robust. Now it became possible, all because of the data that was collected as output from those performed procedures over time. As to explain, output data can be searched for patterns in it, and that pattern further being used for more predictions or determining certain features.

So machine learning is the process of analyzing input data to find patterns in that data and use it further for predictions. Many big companies use this technology in their businesses. Netflix uses it in its recommendation software, where it analyzes our past data and recommends new shows or movies to us. Google uses it in its search engine.

Linear Regression Modeling

Linear regression is considered one of the most well-known algorithms in statistics and machine learning.

Machine learning mainly involves building a model with minimum error and making the predictions accurately as much as possible. So in applied machine learning, we make use of algorithms from many different fields, including statistics.

Linear regression, also known as the straight-line equation, was developed in mathematical statistics and studied as a model for understanding the relationship between input and output variables, and so is found useful in machine learning. So it's both a statistical algorithm and a machine learning algorithm.

Linear regression is a *linear model*, i.e., a model where we have a linear relationship between the input variables "x" and the output variables "y." So mainly, we can determine that linear relationship in equation form and further can find "y" on the availability of "x" or vice-versa.

When we have only two variables (one input variable and one output variable), then this method is referred to as **simple linear regression**. In a simple regression problem (input variable "x" and output variable "y") the equation representing the linear regression model is:

$$y = m * x + c$$

Where m is the slope and c its y-intercept.

Using Inbuilt Linear Regression From Scikit-learn

Let us see how to do it via code example.

from sklearn.linear_model import LinearRegression

 # Training Data and Test Data

```
x_training = [1, 2, 3, 4, 5]

y_training = [1, 9, 0, 4, 5]

x_test = [2, 4, 7, 8, 9]

y_test = [8, 6, 9, 4, 2]
```

 # Classifier Definition

```
clf = LinearRegression()

clf.fit(x_training, y_training)

accuracy = clf.score(x_test, y_test)
```

 # print accuracy of data

```
print(accuracy)
```

Building Own Linear Regression Model

To do that, we need to use fake data for x's and y's, and on that, we need to find Slope "m" and Y-intercept "c."

Import numpy as np

 # creating fake data

xaxis = np.array([3, 2, 1, 9, 5], dtype = np.float64)

yaxis = np.array([5, 8, 6, 4, 6], dtype = np.float64)

Our objective is to find the best-fit line equation. The definition of this equation will be y = mx + c.

The slope, m, of the best-fit line is defined as:

m = (((mean(xaxis) * mean(yaxis)) - mean(xaxis * yaxis)) /

((mean(xaxis) * mean(yaxis)) - mean(xaxis * yaxis)))

The y intercept, c, of the best-fit line is defined as:

c = mean(yaxis) – (m * mean(xaxis))

The resulting best-fit line or regression line is:

regression_line = [(m*x)+c for x in xaxis]

This regression line represents a straight line equation with best-fit slope and Y-intercept values. Now imagine working with a dataset of 2 million data points. Such a scenario requires the need to automatically find out how good our best-fit line or regression line is.

The squared error value helps in finding the error rate.

The equation for that is:

```
def square_error(yaxis_orig,yaxis_line):

    return sum( (yaxis_line - yaxis_orig) * (yaxis_line - yaxis_orig) )

def coefficient_of_determination(yaxis_orig,yaxis_line):

    y_mean_line = [mean(yaxis_orig) for y in yaxis_orig]

    square_error_regr = square_error(yaxis_orig, yaxis_line)

    square_error_y_mean = square_error(yaxis_orig, y_mean_line)

    return 1 - (square_error_regr/square_error_y_mean)
```

The Complete Code

```
Import numpy as np
#creating fake data

        xaxis = np.array([3, 2, 1, 9, 5], dtype = np.float64)

        yaxis = np.array([5, 8, 6, 4, 6], dtype = np.float64)

def slope_and_intercept(xaxis,yaxis):

    m = (((mean(xaxis) * mean(yaxis)) - mean(xaxis * yaxis)) /
```

```
        ((mean(xaxis) * mean(xaxis)) - mean(xaxis * xaxis)))

    c = mean(yaxis) - m*mean(xaxis)

    return m, c

regression_line = [(m*x)+c for x in xaxis]

def square_error(yaxis_orig, yaxis_line):

    return sum( (yaxis_line - yaxis_orig) * (yaxis_line - yaxis_orig) )

def coefficient_of_determination(yaxis_orig, yaxis_line):

    y_mean_line = [mean(yaxis_orig) for y in yaxis_orig]

    square_error_regr = square_error(yaxis_orig, yaxis_line)

    square_error_y_mean = square_error(yaxis_orig, y_mean_line)

    return 1 - (square_error_regr / square_error_y_mean)

m, c = slope_and_intercept(xaxis,yaxis)

regression_line = [(m * x) + c for x in xaxis]

r_square = coefficient_of_determination(yaxis,regression_line)

print(r_square)
```

Data Science Linear Regression Modelling For Titanic Dataset

What is Data Science?

Data science has evolved tremendously in recent years, and it is being used extensively worldwide to get meaningful details from conversations. It also provides an edge to companies over their rivals in a significant manner.

We will analyze the Titanic Disaster people's survival using Machine Learning techniques. We use the Titanic Disaster Dataset to go through each stage of the data science cycle one by one. There are multiple phases present in a Data Science model like Data Extraction, Processing, Visualizing Data, Building the code, evaluating the code, Fine-tuning the prediction models, and Data explosion to the APIs for integration.

Data Science is one of the latest emerging technology in the field of Data mining. With the help of Data Science, we can extract meaningful insights, statistics, and patterns from structured and unstructured data in various forms that can benefit the organization in a significant way. Source for the Data Science can be in any form like Facebook posts, Tweets, Videos or Images, Databases, APIs, Web content, etc.

Forecasting Vs. Predictive Model Vs. Machine Learning

Forecasting is the process of estimating the future occurrence of an event based on the past and present data available, which is usually done at an aggregate level.

Example:

- How many numbers of passengers can we expect in a given flight for a particular class?

- How many customer care calls can we expect in the next 1 hour?

To do at a granular level, we need predictive modeling. **Predictive modeling** used to perform prediction more granular like "Who are the customers who are likely to buy a specific product in next month" and act accordingly. Identify the right customer and act.

Machine Learning is a method of teaching machines to learn things and improve predictions/behavior based on data on their own.

Example:

- Create an algorithm that can power Google search.
- Amazon or Facebook recommendation system.

Data Science Project Cycle Overview

Data science helps us to make a journey from data to valuable insights, but it has several components along the way.

Extract the Data

The first piece is the extract phase. We need to get the data first before we do anything with it. And data extraction, or data acquisition, is the first step towards our data science journey. Data may have to be acquired from one or multiple sources.

Process the Data

Once we have extracted the data, the next building block is to organize or pre-process the data, because rarely you will get data in the required format. You may have to perform various data wrangling tasks to clean it and then put it into the right shape.

Analyze the Data

Once we have organized the data, our next step is to analyze and create a model. In real-world settings, you may have to try different models and then analyze them and evaluate them over and over again until it reaches the desired level.

Present the Data

Once your data analysis part is done, then the next step is to publish the results for visualization. It could be a report or presentation that you may want to show to your stakeholders. It could be a blog or website that you want to put it on the web. It could even be an application that has to be deployed in a production environment.

You may have to repeat this whole cycle again with some new and additional data with different processing or different analysis or modeling techniques, or different approaches of presenting the results. So this outer loop is used to represent the iterative nature of the whole data science cycle. This shows that it is a continuous ongoing activity where you incrementally build upon your previous works.

Data Science Models

Below are the two Data science models that are widely used.

Classification Model

Classification Model is used when an expected result falls under a defined set of possible outcomes.

Example:

1. **Multi-Class Classification**: For a given image, we will classify it correctly as containing Dogs, Cats, etc.

2. **Binary Classification**: Here, we will be given an email to predict if it is a genuine email or spam.

Classification Model Algorithms

a. Decision Trees

b. K Nearest Neighbors

c. Naive Bayes

d. Logistic Regression

Regression Model

The regression model is used when an expected output is represented by a quantity that is continuous in manner. Example: Linear Regression Model

Example:

- Predict housing prices for a given location
- Revenue a customer will generate for a financial year.

Regression Model Algorithms

a. Linear Regression

    b.   Regression Trees (e.g., Random Forest)

Here we will be using this algorithm for the Regression model.

Why Python for Data Science?

1. Python as a language itself is fairly easy to learn, as its syntax is similar to other common languages.

2. Python code is also easy to read and is quite intuitive.

3. Availability of various open-source, free tools, and libraries for various data science-related activities. These tools are very helpful in making a head start with data science projects.

4. A complete ecosystem in Python's stack for data science-related activities right from the extraction phase to the presentation phase of the data science project.

5. Python has a very strong and active community, and you can easily get help if you run across any problem or issue.

6. Python is also quite fast and scalable with respect to some other languages and frameworks that are typically used in the data science world, such as MATLAB or Stata or R.

Setting up Environment

Install Anaconda Distribution

To install the Anaconda distribution on your local machine, you can download the installer from https://www.anaconda.com/download/

1. Click on the download button to download the installer, Save File.

2. Simply double-click on the installer to install the anaconda distribution.

3. Set the installation location. I will let it as the default location.

4. Click Next. From the Advanced Options screen, we want to add Anaconda to the path so that we can access the Anaconda distribution from any terminal in our command prompt, so let's check this box.

5. Click Install to install the Anaconda distribution. So now, Anaconda is completely installed. Click Finish.

6. Let's verify if we have successfully installed the Anaconda distribution. We can use any terminal. I am using the Git Bash terminal. Open the Git Bash terminal and type the command below.

7. Anaconda distribution comes with several pre-installed Python packages, so let's check out the installed Python packages using the conda list command.

Install Jupyter Notebook

Jupyter Notebook will be the working environment for data science projects due to its ability to combine code blocks along with human-friendly text that can be formatted using markdowns. You can also view the images and videos right in your notebook. This makes Jupyter Notebook as a very interactive document, and you can work on it using your favorite web browsers.

Jupyter Notebook not only supports Python kernels, means not only you can run Python code in it, but you can also run codes in other languages as well, such as R or Julia or Scala, right in the single notebook so that you can get all of this in a single development environment.

1. To create Jupyter Notebook, From the Git bash terminal, Type command "jupyter notebook –port 7777," as shown below. By default, the port is 8888.

2. Now Jupyter Notebook opens in a web browser with the port specified.

3. On the Right-hand side, Click New -> Python2 to create a new Jupyter Notebook to build code blocks.

Jupyter Notebook - Basics

The following topics are the basics of getting acquainted with Python programming language.

a. Understanding Operators

b. Variables and Data Types

c. Conditional Statements

d. Looping Constructs

e. Functions

     f.   Data Structure

     g.   Lists

     h.   Dictionaries

     i.   Understanding Standard Libraries in Python

     j.   Reading a CSV File in Python

1. Click a cell, write simple python code.

2. Click Shift + enter, to execute the cell, and the notebook prints the output.

Setting Up Cookiecutter Data Science Project Template

1. To set up a Data Science project, we need to install the Cookiecutter template.

2. Since we have installed Anaconda distribution, we can use conda install command to install the cookiecutter project template. To install, execute the following command in Git bash terminal *"conda install cookiecutter."* This will install cookiecutter locally

3. To clone the project structure from GitHub to your local machine. Navigate your path to the project folder in Git Bash terminal and type the below command and press Enter

"cookiecutter http://github.com/drivendata/cookiecutter-data-science."

4. While cloning, few project description has to be provided like Project name, Author, Description.

5. After successful cloning, you can view the folder structure of the project. To view, type below command and press Enter.

"tree –L 3."

Add Project to Versioning System

First, ensure you are on the project root folder path in the Git Bash Terminal. Below are the commands to perform versioning activities for the project.

git init	Initialize an empty Git repository
git status	Lists the pending changes to be committed
git add.	Adds changes to versioning system (. Dot specifies push all files)
git commit -m ' Message for commit. '	Commit the changes with a message
git log – oneline	Lists all the commit logs

Extracting Data

Data can come from different types of sources, and there are Python libraries available to extract the data. The data acquisition can be made in any of the below ways,

1. Extracting Data from Databases (SQLite, MySQL, SQL Server)

2. Extracting Data Through APIs

3. Extracting Data Using Web Scraping

4. Extracting Data from Files in a shared path

Many websites host popular datasets from the ML perspective for data science projects. Ex: http://www.data.gov, Amazon AWS, etc.

In our case, for data science analysis, we are manually downloading an excel type dataset named Titanic Dataset from kaggle.com. (Downloading of excel can also be done programmatically using Python code). Download the test.csv, train.csv files to the data\raw folder path in the project workspace.

Exploratory Data Analysis

In probing the data set, we will look into four steps:

- **Extract the data**: To load the dataset.

- **Clean the data**: To find and fill/correct the missing values.

- **Plot the data**: To create graphs and charts that will identify correlations and hidden insights out of the data.

We will be using two sets of datasets, one for Training and another to Test. The training dataset is used to build our predictive model and the Test data to manipulate and generate an output file.

Let's first look at loading the Training data set.

1. Import below Python libraries

- Pandas: Pandas, aka "Python Data Analysis Library" used for data manipulation.

- Numpy: NumPy supports multi-dimensional arrays and matrices computation.

- OS: Operating system User environments

We have loaded the dataset and converted it to DataFrame. Python libraries use DataFrame as an object to manipulate on rows and columns of the dataset. From the above figure, we can see the **Survived** column, which will be our desired column. If Survival equals 1, it means the passenger is survived, else the passenger has not survived the disaster.

Below are the column attributes that describe the passengers in the Titanic dataset.

- PassengerId: Unique id for the passenger in the dataset

- Pclass: Class of the passenger (1st class, 2nd class, 3rd class).

- Name: Passenger Name

- Sex: Sex of the Passenger (Male, Female)

- Age: Passenger age

- SibSp: Count of siblings and spouses traveling along with the passenger

- Parch: Count of parents and children traveling along with the passenger

- Ticket: Ticket number

- Fare: Ticket Fare Amount

- Cabin: Cabin number of the Passenger

- Embarked: Location passenger boarded. Three possible values S, C, Q

Now, we are going to concatenate Train.csv & Test.csv dataset, Add **Survived** column with the default value (i.e., -888) to maintain the same column structure.

Pandas allow getting the high-level summary of columns in the data frame using the **describe** method. This function applies and works only for numeric columns. For non-numeric convert, the column type to numeric explicitly and apply the function.

Feature Engineering

In our earlier section, on querying and probing, we found some data correlation and patterns pertaining to the Titanic dataset, but still, there are more features to analyze.

Feature Engineering is the transforming of raw data to better representative features, which can be fed to machine learning algorithms.

- Title: Extract the Title from Passenger Name like Mr. Miss Dr. etc.

- AgeState: Fill the missing ages to the Training dataset using the train set, and we fill in ages in the Test dataset using values calculated from the Training set as well.

- Fare: Set missing Fare value by the average fare using the MEAN function.

- Embark: Set missing values of Embarked with the most frequent Embarked value

- Cabin: Set NaN values with U (i.e., Unknown). Extract the first letter of the Cabin column and set the value

- Is Mother: Set 1 or 0, Lady more than age 18 and is married (not miss).

- Is Male: Set values male = 1 and female = 0.

- FamilySize: Count of relatives pertaining to the passenger (inclusive of self).

After feature engineering, we are now ready to save the processed dataset to the project folder path "**data\processed**" that has been picked and transformed from the raw data folder (**data\raw**).

Building and Evaluating Predictive Model

To build and evaluate the predictive model, the below steps are followed.

1. Split the concatenated dataset into two data frames, namely TRAIN and TEST.

2. A TRAIN data frame is used to build a predictive model, and TEST is to evaluate.

3. Assess the predictive model using the TRAIN data frameset.

4. Validate the model using the TEST set and generate the output file.

Repeat steps 2 and 3 until a desired output score of the model is achieved.

Prepare the Processed Data for Machine Learning Model

- Import the processed data files from the data/Processed folder (train.csv, test.csv) and put it into two data frames, namely test_data_frame (test_df) and train_data_frame (train_df).

- Most of the machine learning algorithms expect numerical arrays; hence here we are creating two arrays, one for input and another for output.

- Create array X, by fetching all rows and all columns EXCEPT the Survived column.

- Now let's split the array X into two parts, one for the training the model and another for evaluating our model performance.

Create Baseline Model

1. Before we feed data to our model, lets first build our Baseline model, the accuracy score output is 61%.

2. Submit the Baseline model predicted file to an external folder (*data/external*).

Create Logic Regression Model

Create Logic Regression Model.

Call the *SubmitFile* function to write the predicted dummy file to the external folder (*data/external*).

Chapter 5

Machine Learning and Deep Learning Using Python

Machine Learning and Deep Learning Using Python

To loosely speak Machine learning is a computer program that analyses a collection of data to predict future changes and adapt accordingly. Whereas automation is a concept where repetitive tasks are performed through a computer program without any human effort. Automation, on its own, cannot adjust to any changes in the application on which tasks are performed. No future prediction is carried out in automation.

Type of Machine Learning

Machine learning can be primarily classified into three types:

1. Supervised machine learning.

2. Unsupervised machine learning.

3. Reinforcement machine learning.

Supervised Machine Learning

In simple words, supervised machine learning is a program designed with machine learning algorithms that are trained with a huge amount of data related to any problem or task and depending upon the training, it tries to predict the future outcome, which runs with real-time data.

Suppose we have a process that takes X as input and provides Y as output.

We collect test data and output of the application for a certain amount of time so that the data collection consists of varied types of scenarios.

Then we are training our machine learning program (i.e., a program designed with machine learning algorithms) on this data. This is called supervised learning-based. The data trained our program to gain the ability to predict the future outcome of the process based on the real-time data we provide.

Advantages:

- This method can be really useful in analysis stock exchange to predict outcomes in the future.

- It's useful when we huge amount of available test data from the past run and can use the same to predict the future through supervised learning.

Unsupervised Machine Learning

In simple words, unsupervised learning is an analysis of a huge amount of data without any programmer supervision to predict clustering and association in the data.

This type of training is really useful when trying to analyze customer's behavior in insurance/marketing sections to predict which base of users can be attracted to which product/policy.

Unsupervised machine learning can be classified into below types:

- **Clustering:** Discover groupings in data such as classification of human cells to cancerous and non-cancerous types, classification of consumer base by grouping them based on their marketing activities.

- **Association:** Association is a technique using which new rules are generated to find data sets that share some common properties.

Reinforcement Machine Learning

Reinforcement is a branch of machine learning where software is learning from trial and error and automatically determine ideal behavior within a specific context to provide maximum output. This type of learning is usually not recommended as its memory expensive as it stores each outcome based on the scenario, and if the scenarios are too complex, then memory usage is high.

Predictive Analysis in Python

Let us see the step by step details on performing Predictive Analysis using Python.

Step - 1

Import necessary libraries like pandas, sklearn, and metrics.

```
#Import necessary models:
from sklearn import metrics
import pandas as p
from sklearn.tree import DecisionTreeClassifier
from sklearn.ensemble import RandomForestClassifier
from sklearn.linear_model import LogisticRegression
from sklearn.preprocessing import LabelEncoder
```

Step – 2

Read the dataset (Data on which prediction needs to be done). For the sake of simplicity, a CSV dataset with a sample of 25 records has been taken. Out of these 25 records, 20 records would be used to train the model. And for the rest of the five records, the prediction will be made.

ID, Gender, Relationship, Income, Loan_Amt, Approval_Status

    1, M, Y, 20000, 49000, Y

    2, M, Y, 11000, 17000, N

    3, M, N, 2200, 97725, N

4, M, N, 17544, 40156, Y

5, F, Y, 29008, 62444, Y

6, F, Y, 7000, 97000, N

7, F, Y, 19562, 62000, Y

8, F, Y, 10500, 47000, Y

9, F, N, 1000, 79000, N

10, M, N, 10000, 88000, N

11, M, Y, 26000, 82000, Y

12, M, Y, 28000, 29000, Y

13, M, N, 6000, 73000, N

14, F, N, 28000, 68000, Y

15, F, Y, 10000, 9000, Y

16, F, Y, 27000, 900000, N

17, M, N, 21000, 700000, N

18, M, Y, 7000, 5000, Y

19, M, N, 13800, 600000, N

20, F, N, 24300, 31000, Y

21, M, N, 26000, 74000, Y

22, M, Y, 25000, 70000, N

23, M, Y, 25000, 99000, Y

24, F, N, 28000, 44000, Y

25, F, Y, 17142, 34000, Y

Information about the Data

ID	Gender	Relationship	Income	Loan_Amt	Approval_Status
1	M	Y	20000	49000	Y
2	M	Y	11000	17000	N
3	M	N	2200	97725	N
4	M	N	17544	40156	Y
5	F	Y	29008	62444	Y
6	F	Y	7000	97000	N
7	F	Y	19562	62000	Y
8	F	Y	10500	47000	Y
9	F	N	1000	79000	N
10	M	N	10000	88000	N

The above table shows the sample dummy data. Whether the loan for a particular person is approved or not is dependent on its Gender, relationship, and Income.

```
#Read the data from the csv file using Pandas
data = p.read_csv("path/file.csv")
```

Step – 3

A predictive model only accepts numerical data. Hence all the Non-Numeric columns should be converted to Numeric columns. This can be done using:

```
#Encoding Non-Numeric Values
encode = LabelEncoder()
cols = ['Status','Gender','Relationship']
for colnm in cols:
        data[colnm] = encode.fit_transform(data[colnm])
```

Step – 4

Splitting training data and test data.

train_data = data.head(20)

test_data = data.head(5)

Step – 4

Defining the below.

Input variables which will be feed to the model, or in other words which will be used to train the model to predict the output

The output variable is the one which we suppose model to predict its value.

```
#Defining Input variables and Output variables
ipvar = ['Gender','Income','Loan_Amt']
opvar = ['Approval_Status']
```

Step – 5

Defining the model.

```
#Defining the Model
model = RandomForestClassifier(n_estimators=100)
#model = DecisionTreeClassifier()  /* You can try with different models and check the accuracy */
#model = LogisticRegression()      /* You can try with different models and check the accuracy */
```

Step – 6

Training the Model using training data.

```
#Training the Model using Training data
model.fit(train_data[ipvar],train_data[opvar])
```

Applying the test data on the trained model and predicting the output of test data.

```
#Applying the test data on the trained model and predicting the output
prediction = model.predict(test_data[ipvar])
```

Step – 7

Check the values predicted by the Model.

```
#Checking the Predicted Values
for values in prediction:
        print(values)
```

Checking the accuracy by comparing predicted values and actual values.

```
#Checking the Accuracy of the predicted data by comparing it with Actual Output
accuracy = metrics.accuracy_score(prediction,test_data[opvar])
```

Try feeding the data to different models and check the output. (Step-6)

Code Snippet

from sklearn.linear_model import LogisticRegression

from sklearn.preprocessing import LabelEncoder

Read the data from the csv file using Pandas

data = p.read_csv("path/file.csv")

Encoding Non-Numeric Values

encode = LabelEncoder()

cols = ['Status','Gender','Relationship']

for colnm in cols:

    data[colnm] = encode.fit_transform(data[colnm])

Splitting Training data and Test data

train_data = data.head(20)

test_data = data.tail(5)

Defining Input variables and Output variables

```python
ipvar = ['Gender','Income','Loan_Amt']

opvar = ['Approval_Status']

#Defining the Model

model = RandomForestClassifier(n_estimators=100)

# model = DecisionTreeClassifier()  /* You can try with different
models and check the accuracy */

# model = LogisticRegression()       /* You can try with different
models and check the accuracy */

# Training the Model using Training data

model.fit(train_data[ipvar],train_data[opvar])

# Applying the test data on the trained model and predicting the
output

prediction = model.predict(test_data[ipvar])

# Checking the Predicted Values

for values in prediction:

    print(values)

# Checking the Accuracy of the predicted data by comparing it with
Actual Output

accuracy = metrics.accuracy_score(prediction,test_data[opvar]
```

Table of Content (For Reference)

ID	Gender	Relationship	Income	Loan_Amt	Approval_Status
1	M	Y	20000	49000	Y
2	M	Y	11000	17000	N
3	M	N	2200	97725	N
4	M	N	17544	40156	Y
5	F	Y	29008	62444	Y
6	F	Y	7000	97000	N
7	F	Y	19562	62000	Y
8	F	Y	10500	47000	Y
9	F	N	1000	79000	N
10	M	N	10000	88000	N
11	M	Y	26000	82000	Y
12	M	Y	28000	29000	Y
13	M	N	6000	73000	N
14	F	N	28000	68000	Y
15	F	Y	10000	9000	Y
16	F	Y	27000	900000	N

17	M	N	21000	700000	N
18	M	Y	7000	5000	Y
19	M	N	13800	600000	N
20	F	N	24300	31000	Y
21	M	N	26000	74000	Y
22	M	Y	25000	700000	N
23	M	Y	25000	99000	Y
24	F	N	28000	44000	Y
25	F	Y	17142	34000	Y

Chapter 6

Machine Learning Approach in Python with Random Forest Model

To analyze and present the CSV data in a better manner so that we can get visual or pictorial presentation for clear understanding of the data depicted in the comma-separated value which can be processed in python environment so that data analysis can be done using any standard algorithm-RandomForest and we can present the data in useful manner displayed and arranged.

Need for Cross-Validation

The current need for **Cross-Validation** of machine learning is as follows:

- There is no direct approach available to analyze the current machine learning model being used in the analysis

- There is a need for cross-validation of current Machine learning models being used, keeping in mind that every model may not be suitable to the solution with the elapsed time period and varying nature of datasets; it's better to cross-validate them so that we can better predict using the ML models.

Cross-Validation Process Flow Pipeline

The following is a process flow for the **Cross-Validation** and analysis in the python environment. We need to have Python to be installed as preliminary essentials for the cross-validation technique to be implemented.

1. First of all, we need to have healthcare diagnosis data in CSV format.

2. Then using any standard read() method, we can read the file using Python script.

3. Data analysis can be done using any standard algorithm present in Python packages(RandomForestClassifier)

4. Then we can create/update CSV data to be displayed as a meaningful dashboard.

5. We can append the analyzed result as a new column as Avg failures or summation.

6. Data analysis can be done using any standard algorithm present in Python packages.

The analysis will be done using the Models of Python and once the output is predicted will be stored in CSV File with a new column/table/view from which decision and prediction or reporting can be done easily with Python Graph Plotting library like (Matlab Plot) to display the values in easy to understand manner.

Machine Learning Concept

Machine learning is the new era of computer programing that can be automatically used for a processor to learn and implement something from the teaching without being programmed by the developer on the fly. Machine learning concept is nothing but the development of computer routines that can utilize pre-gathered datasets and utilize the same for the benefit for decision-making purposes, which usually done by human beings.

There are few algorithms and mathematical expressions and even statistical analysis tools that can be combined with Machine Learning so that software applications can serve for prediction outcomes without using programs by developers. The basic intention of machine learning is to utilize algorithms that can intake few pre-existing datasets and use math/statistical analysis methods, data mining or predictive modeling methods to predict some reasonable outcomes while deciding outputs as new data becomes feedback to the Model.

These ML methods actually require analyzing through data to look for a similar type of recordset and adjust the program actions as per the need. Example of real machine learning is from shopping data on the internet and being served ads related to their purchase.

Files Required

1. CSV file with Diagnosis Healthcare Data

2. Python Script file to process the Data and Create the pictorial or graphical presentation out of the results analyzed

Python Script Preparation

Here is the script for connecting to the backend and reading data from the CSV file using the standard readfile() method in Python.

Step1: Importing Essential libraries for Python

The following library has to be imported

```
from sklearn import metrics
import pandas as p
from sklearn.tree import DecisionTreeClassifier
from sklearn.ensemble import RandomForestClassifier
from sklearn.linear_model import LogisticRegression
from sklearn.preprocessing import LabelEncoder
```

Step-2: In this step Python script reads data from the CSV file

import csv

data = p.read_csv("C:\input\sample.csv")

Step-3: Handling the Non-numeric values in Prediction process

encode = LabelEncoder()

cols = ['Gender']

for colnm in cols:

data[colnm] = encode.fit_transform(data[colnm])

Step-4: Splitting the data into Train data & Test Data and defining Input and output variable

train_data = data.head(20)

test_data = data.tail(5)

```
ipvar = ['Gender','Factor1','Factor2','Factor3']

opvar = ['Diagnosis_Status']
```

Step-5: Defining the Machine Learning Model and providing input

```
model = RandomForestClassifier(n_estimators=100)

model.fit(train_data[ipvar],train_data[opvar])
```

Step-6: Predicting the Output & finding the accuracy of the Model

```
prediction = model.predict(test_data[ipvar])

for values in prediction:

    print(values)

accuracy_calculator = metrics.accuracy_score(prediction,test_data[opvar])
```

Graph showing the cross validation analysis process in Python for RandomForestClassifier model

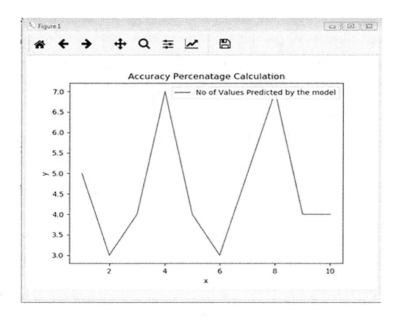

Depiction from Graph

From the graph plotted in Python using the Matplot library, we can find out the accuracy percentage of one of the Machine Learning models (Random Forest Classifier) that this model is predicting the values of the numbers that have been predicted with accuracy by use of the cross-validation technique. So it can be implemented in real-time problem solving and prediction purposes with respect to the next execution by using train data as test data.

This can prove that the ML model is functioning well as per expectation.

Conclusion

Usually, we go for an ML model selection on the basis of prior experience or by the advice of experience or the guesswork, which is not valid for all problem-solving models. Though it may fit for the problem for some time till the time factor comes into play and we find the prediction is not accurate. This is usually a problem for many ML implementation. We can cross-validate any ML model before its implemented for problem-solving. The above approach explained has evaluated one model with Healthcare data to find the accuracy percentage, and from a graphical presentation, we can decide whether the model is accurate or not using cross-validation. A similar approach can be taken so that we can cross-validate other models like DecisionTreeClassifier and Logistic Regression models.

Application of Machine Learning in Automation

Although automation helps speed up completion of repetitive tasks, it lacks the capability of adapting to future changes arising due to changes in business requirements and application enhancements. Hence from time to time, maintenance of automation scripts is required to meet the client's needs.

To overcome these challenges, we will be implementing machine learning practices in automation so that the automation script can auto adapt to business changes to some extent and avoid human maintenance efforts.

Common Machine Learning Algorithms

Below is the list of commonly used algorithms in machine learning. They can be used in almost any data problem.

Linear Regression

We calculate the real values of any substance by processing continuous dependent and independent variables. The best line is plotted by calculating the relationship between the dependent variable and the independent variable.

The best line is known as the regression line and is calculated by using the following linear equation.

Dependent Variable = Slope * Independent variable + Intercept

Types of Linear Regression:

- Simple Linear Regression: In this regression, only one independent variable is involved in the calculation of the regression line.

- Multiple Linear Regression: In this regression, only two or more independent variables are involved in the calculation of the regression line.

Logistic Regression

The estimation of discrete values, i.e., 0 and 1, based on independent variables considered in logistic regression. It predicts/assume the probability of a repeated event by attaching data into logit function. As it predicts probability, therefore the output values are always within 0 and 1.

KNN Clustering

This is classified as the class of the majority of its nearest neighbors. In simple words, if you are similar to your neighbors, then you are one of them. Or if one looks more similar to one family, then it may belong to it.

Multiple distance functions are available and can be used to predict K Nearest neighbor.

K-Means Clustering

K-mean clustering is a method to create the desired number of partitions of a data set. Partitions mean a set of samples in the data which are most similar to each other. Here the number of partitions can be driven by the user.

Random Forest

We can produce a Random Forest by combining a bunch of decision set. The Random Forest and Isolation Forest fall under the category of ensemble methods. It can also combine the prediction of each tree and vote- the highest voted prediction, which emerges as the final prediction Dimensionality Reduction Algorithms.

Transfer Learning

Transfer learning is a vital problem statement in the current machine learning platform. Which focus on accumulating knowledge while solving one problem and apply the same in a different related problem. For example, the knowledge gained while learning one form of bird can be used while learning a new form of a bird.

VP Tree

VP tree allows the ability to partition data in n-dimensional metric space efficiently. It is more specifically a metric tree. VP tree has the ability to partition data in dimensional space efficiently. Each node of the VP tree stores five crucial pieces of information. They are as follows:

- Data
- Vantage point
- A radius value defining the range of the node
- The left subtree
- The right subtree

Decision Tree

Decision Tree is the most popularly used machine learning algorithm as they are easy to interpret, easy to operationalize, and easy to use. Decision Trees are an important type of algorithm for predictive modeling machine learning. They help in the automatic handling of missing values by taking continuous and categorical inputs. The most common implementation of a decision tree is CART - Classification and Regression Trees.

Classification and Regression Trees

It focuses on accurate assessment when data is noisy (outliers and missing values).

SVM

Support Vector machines developed during the 1990s and became very popular during the 2000s and are most widely used for classification and regression analysis. It defines decision boundaries based on the concept of decision planes. The decision plane separates between a set of objects which have different class memberships. It is implemented using a kernel that helps in linear analysis of the problem statement.

Machine Learning Application in Automation

There are multiple ways machine learning can be implemented in automation to enhance the automation efficiency.

- Utilization of natural language processing in automation can take automation to the next level. Through natural language processing, automation script can understand acceptance criteria and accordingly design test scenarios/cucumber feature scenarios. Hence reducing the workload of going through acceptance criteria and creation of test cases manually.

- Report analysis can be enhanced using machine learning. Using natural language processing and tools such as Word2Vec, automation scripts can be configured to generate reports by analyzing exceptions encountered during the script run. Accordingly, suggestions can be generated to end-user.

- Normally Sikuli is used to perform image validation, and validation takes place by comparing preexisting images with the latest captured image. In this scenario, the major demerit is comparison failure due to differences in pixel. This issue can be efficiently addressed using deep learning algorithms (e.g., Inception developed by Google) to identify varied types of images on which the library is pre-trained to predict.

- Auto new object identification: In most of the automation tools like (UFT, RFT) automation scripts are created based on predefined object repositories. So the user has to identify new objects and create object repositories manually. This is a complex and lengthy task when the new and huge application is involved. Machine learning can be used in this scenario to auto-identify objects that possess a set of predefined characteristics. This can reduce human intervention significantly.

Limitations of this Tool

- Machine learning is a new and complex branch that needs a lot of user experience to work on.

- It cannot be used in every circumstance as they can be solved quickly using traditional programming techniques.

- Needs an amount of data for training in the initial phase, so it can be difficult to implement in new scenarios where previous data is not available.

Conclusion

As humans evolved by their learning and experience through ages, similarly, machines can also be trained to evolve. Automation, which is dominated in the current digital age, has a limitation, and it cannot evolve as per new/existing changes in test application based on existing script strategy and hence machine learning can make this possible and reduce human intervention to a great extent.:

Chapter 7

Bulk Image Compression Using Python

Introduction

It has been rightly said: "A picture is worth a thousand words." We love to interact with images. In fact, our brain is programmed to react faster to visuals than text. The importance of images is increasing over time and whether it is e-commerce, marketing, media or travel, visual graphics – the dominance of images can be seen in the entire sector.

According to HTTP Archive, on an average, around **64%** of a website's weight is comprised of images; this is equivalent to almost **three-fourths** of the data that travels along. An image has the power to grab attention, to tell a story or to convey a message quickly.

Issues with Image Size and their Resolution

Despite all these, one key challenge that we often face is the issue with image size and image quality.

Due to the large size of images, our devices like mobile phones and computers often run out of memory, and sometimes, due to heavy resolution and large size, we also face trouble while opening the image. None to say, it finally slows down our devices.

Even while browsing any website, we often wait for a long time for an image to get uploaded or downloaded, which consumes a large amount of time that costs a lot in today's busy world.

These all are the common problems that every individual faces in today's world.

Proposed Solution

One great solution for all the above issues is **IMAGE OPTIMIZATION**. Image Optimization means reducing the size of an image without affecting its quality.

Image optimization can be achieved through various ways like by visiting the image resizing website, or by using image modifying tools like CompressNow, Optimizilla, JPEG Optimizer, etc.

We can even use a simple Python Program to reduce the size of the image. The below mentioned Python program can iterate through all the images present in a folder and can reduce the size of the images present in the given folder. Here, we can specify the minimum size limit below which the image should not be compressed, and we can mention the quality by which we want to reduce the image size. This can be achieved by using two simple libraries of Python.

PIL: It stands for Python programming language. It is used for opening, manipulating, and saving different image file formats[1].

OS: This module uses the operating system dependent functionality. The *os* and *os.path* modules contain many functions for interacting with the file system[2].

The below code is a simple example to show how Python can be used in image optimization.

Editable Mode:

```python
from PIL import Image

import os

matching_files = []

errors = []

root = input("Enter the root : ")

min_size_for_compression = int(input("Enter the minimum size of image to be compressed (IN BYTES) : "))

for path, subdirs, files in os.walk(root):

    for name in files:

        matching_files.append(os.path.join(path, name))

        print(path, end = ' ')
```

```python
        print(name)

input("\n\nList of all files in the given location obtained.
Press enter to start compression: ")

for image in matching_files:

    try:

        if os.path.getsize(image) > min_size_for_compression:

            im = Image.open(image)

            im.save(image, format = "JPEG", quality = 50)

            print("{} compressed.".format(image))

        else:

            print("{} skipped from compression. File size already
less than given minimum".format(image))

    except Exception as e:

        print("{} had following error : {}".format(image, e))

        errors.append(image)

if len(errors) > 0:

    print("\n\n{} files could not be processed. They are:
\n".format(len(errors)))
```

```
for item in errors:

    print(item)

else:

    print("\n\n All files processed successfully.")
```

Code Walkthrough

The below lines are for importing the modules.

Here PIL and os are imported so that we can use the inbuilt libraries in our coding.

```
from PIL import Image

import os
```

This list is created to store the path of images.

```
matching_files = []
```

This list is to store the errors that may come while reducing the image size.
```
errors = []
```

Here the user is asked to enter the root, i.e., the folder path which contains all the images that the user wants to compress.

```
root = input("Enter the root : ")
```

Here the user is asked to mention a minimum size in bytes below, which we don't want to compress the image.

min_size_for_compression = int(input("Enter the minimum size of image to be compressed (IN BYTES) : "))

Here the path of each image present in the root location is appended in the matching_files list. And we can see the number of images that our Python program is going to compress.

```
for path, subdirs, files in os.walk(root)

    for name in files:

        matching_files.append(os.path.join(path, name))

        print(path, end=' ')

        print(name)
```

Here the user is asked to press enter if he wants to continue with the size reduction.

input("\n\n List of all files in the given location obtained. Press enter to start compression: ")

Here the size of the image is compared with the minimum size given by the user below, which the image should not be compressed. In case the size of the image present in our root folder is greater than the minimum size, then the image will be compressed by the quality mentioned below by the user.

```
for an image in matching_files:

    try:

        if os.path.getsize(image) > min_size_for_compression:

        im = Image.open(image)

        im.save(image, format = "JPEG", quality = 50)

        print("{} compressed.".format(image))
```

Here the images are compressed and saved in the same root location.

Image compression will not happen if the size of the image present in the root folder is less than the minimum size mentioned by the user.

```
        else:

        print("{} skipped from compression. File size already
less than given minimum".format(image))
```

Here all kind of errors are tackled. All the errors are stored in the error[] list.

```
    except Exception as e:

        print("{} had following error : {}".format(image, e))

        errors.append(image)
```

So, the above program shows how Python can be used to get rid of one common issue that we face with images.

The above idea can be used further for video compression too and similarly can be used to play with visual graphics dimensions and resolutions.

Similarly, in many ways, Python can help in making our life easy and simple.

Front End Gui Based Testing

Testing via Pixel Based Comparison Algorithm

This section is about sharing of knowledge on using the traditional image processing algorithm and classification category neural network algorithm in validating the front end, like the logo or the front end info between two different environments. This has been implemented and used as a major component of an automation framework for ETL regression. This concept can be adopted and can be used under any IBU where the front end GUI validation is required.

Application of GUI Based Validation

- Regression is always about the comparison of expected vs. actual. Either an expected logo of a report is compared with the actual logo capture from a report in the same test environment.

- Sometimes it can be a comparison between the image of 2 different environments like UAT and QA

- This can be even used in image-based visual objects, where based on the object availability, certain sets of code would be executed. It's the image-based object coding logic behind QTP.

Used whenever we are not able to capture the object. We create visual object-based coding.

Basic Operation

1. Image Comparison
2. Pattern recognition

To perform this basic operation. Some other image processing algorithm is used in various situation.

For example:

When a programmer intends to make his code wait unless the save button is available on the screen.

The simple straight forward approach is to capture the visual object and wait unless it appears.

But to perform this operation, we make a comparison on the visual object we are capturing on the screen, with the visual object stored in the repository. (Image Comparison Algorithm is used). To capture a visual object, either the entire screen is captured and uses the edge detection algorithm of a square, or we will be cropping the image info from the stored x/y position of the screen.

To accelerate the speed of processing, we can convert the image to lower information by (Image color inversion algorithm, where the entire data can be stored in 2 x 2 matrixes as binary bits.

Even the image resizing algorithm to reduce the size of the image and perform the comparison in low memory.

The Popular Image Processing Algorithm

1. Pixel Based Image Comparison

We fetch the pixel info based on the width and height and do one to one comparison.

Implementation of the logic looks like this

    Image_identical_status_flag=true

    For i = 0 To image_width - 1

        For j = 0 To image_height - 1

            If picture1.Point(x, y) <> picture2.Point(x, y) Then

                Image_identical_status_flag = false

        Exit for

            End if

            Next j

        Next i

We can use this same algorithm even to highlight exactly under which area its differing with little modification.

For i = 0 To image_width - 1

    For j = 0 To image_height - 1

        If picture1.Point(x, y) = picture2.Point(x, y) Then

Picture3.set_pixel(x,y)=white

Else

Picture3.set_pixel(x, y) = red

        End if

        Next j

    Next i

Cropping

Similarly, cropping is about capturing the pixel info between 2 x, y coordinates in a large image, and where the dimension is a decision that can be skipped if the area of the crop is decided with gdi32 base API functions.

Deteriorate the Resolution

Just delete half the pixel information of the color like 255 is the pixel color makes it as 55. In such a way, the resolution will be diminished and looks like a blurred picture

Heuristic Thresh Holding is an algorithm where we have to identify the common color of an image and make it as a thresh hold. Simply by dividing, it results in a black and white image, which can be used in pattern recognition easily, explained in the below topic.

Color Image Inversion is 255-current pixel value = new pixel value, which gives the grayscale pattern.

Bright/Darkness Make it more dark or bright, can be used to highlight the edges more specific and helps in edge detection algorithm.

- If current_pixel + 10 > 255 then current_pixel = 255 else 0

- If current_pixel + 10 > 255 then current_pixel = current_pixel + 255 else nothing

- So on.

Edge Detection Logic

    a. Get the entire pixel by pixel info of a picture.

    b. It will be analyzing all the 8 pixels which are surrounding it.

    c. Find the darkest and lightest pixel color.

    d. if (-) (lightest_pixel_value - darkest_pixel_value) < threshold)

then the pixel will be rewritten as 1;

else the pixel will be rewritten as 0;

Now, the image border is detected in 0, 1 pattern used in pattern recognition neural network algorithm.

Pattern Recognition

It's another popular area which is used to determine the handwriting or voice recognition, where we use it to recognize a similar pattern. The best algorithm used for this job where prediction and self-analyzable program, which can determine the pattern is Neural Network algorithm.

Here we will discuss how we use the image processing algorithm in pattern recognition using the base concept of neural network.

Brief Info on Neural Network

1. A neural network is an evolutionary algorithm, which is a replica of a biological neuron, used in the field of AI and proven in many areas of classification and grouping. The majorly applied areas are handwriting recognition, voice recognition, and Games AI bots training.

2. Generally, training a neural network takes time. But the hopping algorithm used in the Network algorithm is the straight forward and simplest network for pattern recognizing.

3. To get a little understanding of neural networks, here is an example.

Logical gates are the base component of building a processor and processor are the brain of a PC where the logical base gates are driven by the gates of "AND," "NOT," "OR," and "XOR" so on.

Neural networks can be used to create this kind of logical gates any time dynamically at anywhere in the network region. Similar to human understanding, based on changing threshold values, the gates appear in a different area of the network and work as an independent programing language automatically.

Here is a simple example of the logical gate derivation.

i.   When we input 1 and 1, it is added as 2, which is greater than threshhold 1.5, so it results in 1.

ii.   When we input 1 and 0, the added result is 1, which is not greater than 1, i.e., 0 is the output.

iii.   Similar to the above 2nd point 0 and 1 results the same.

iv.   0 and 0 will also be lesser then threshhold 1.5, resulting in zero.

Similarly, for the same neural network, if we set the threshhold to 0.9, we will get the output of OR Logic.

Consider a network that feedback on itself, changing the thresh hold value.

That's how the trick works. **Hopping algorithm** is a similar pattern, where we make the neural network recognize what input we are giving in and form the pathway. After that, when a similar pattern is inserted, it will activate the neural output, which is the base logic for pattern recognizing.

A neural network is implemented with the base matrix concept, where the neural connection is defined in the dimension of a matrix. To implement this, we have to perform an operation on mathematical matrices and apply the thresh hold logic — Via which it can recognize the pattern.

How to Implement Hopping Neural Network in Image Pattern Recognizing

1. We will be using the image mentioned above processing algorithm to convert two images into the same size.

Preference is given to smaller width and height image, and the larger image is resized.

2. Using the color inversion\heuristic threshold technique\image edge pattern is recognized and converted into black and white, i.e., 0, 1 pattern.

3. These patterns are trained in a neural network, to be recognized, where it will be activated even when the image is inverted or similar. Such that we can recognize the pattern of the image.

Perception of Artificial Intelligence

Generally, human being perceives their environment through different channels such as sight, sound, touch, smell, and taste. Similarly, it is possible to make robots perceive information through different methods. Perception is one of the main processes in robot development.

Perception involves interpreting the data received through various channels like vision, speech, and touch. Robots use exotic sensors such as laser rangefinders, speedometers, and radar to process auditory and visual information from the world. The main channels used by Robots for perceiving information are vision and spoken language that drives problem-solving behaviors.

Vision

A video camera provides a computer with visual information from the real world. But in reality, it is a challenge to interpret the captured images from the camera. The vision computes the visual information it receives from outside. Vision creates a 2-D image of the real-world objects by gathering the light scattered from them. Each pixel in the image can hold a single bit of information (either black or white) or many bits (color and intensity information). An image obtained from the video camera encompasses thousands of pixels. Four main operations, in the order of increasing complexity, done with an image, are:

- Signal Processing: Enhancing the image for better interpretation.

- Measurement Analysis: If the image contains a single object, determine the two-dimensional extent of the object.

- Pattern Recognition: Classify the single object image into a category drawn from a finite set of possibilities.

- Image Understanding: Locate the objects in the image containing many objects and building a three dimensional model of the scene.

2-D images are usually indeterminate. But it is practicable to develop any number of 3-D worlds for image creation. Multiple images of the same object enhance the repossession of the 3-D structure of an image. Acquiring multiple concurrent views of an object using two or more cameras is called stereo vision. Moving the camera provides multiple views. We have to acquire the knowledge of how the motion affects the image that gets produced. High-level knowledge is also important for interpreting visual data. Steps involved in standard image understanding are:

1. Conversion of the analog video signal into a digital image.

2. Extraction of image features like edges and regions using an efficient algorithm. Edges are curves in the image plane across which there is a substantial change in the image brightness. Edge detection helps in building an idealized line. The reason is that the edge contours in the image correspond to important scene contours.

3. Compute the Orientations. This involves linking the detected pixels that belong to the same edge curves. This can be done by assuming that any two neighboring pixels that are both edge pixels with consistent orientation must belong to the same edge curve.

4. Combine surfaces into 3-D solids

5. Group smaller solids into large 3-D composite objects.

6. Match the entities against the knowledge base for selecting the most appropriate interpretation for the image.

3-D Information Extraction Using Vision

For performing manipulation, navigation, and recognition, the extraction of 3-D information of the image is essential. Given below are the three major aspects of this:

- The scene is segmented into individual objects.

- For each object, determine the position and orientation relative to the observer.

- For each object, determine the shape.

The process of organizing the array of image pixel into regions which correspond to the semantically meaningful objects in the scene is known as the segmentation. Edge detection is a very beneficial method in the image and scene segmentation, but it is not sufficient by itself. The reasons behind that are:

1. Detection of edge curves in surface boundaries is difficult due to their low contrast.

2. Edge curves detected may also contain noise, markings, or shadows.

Segmentation maximizes the extraction of 3-D information about the scene. For performing manipulation and navigation tasks, it is vital to determine the pose of the object which is done by finding the position and orientation of an object relative to the observer. A control loop setting is used to accomplish manipulation and navigation tasks. Feedback provided by the sensory information modifies the motion of the robot. The change in the object's distance and its orientation aids in shape determination of the object. Orientation can be applied in two senses:

1. The orientation of the object as a whole, which can be expressed in terms of 3-D rotation relating its coordinate frame to that of the camera.

2. The surface orientation of the object at a point, which can be expressed by a vector that gives the direction of the unit surface normal vector, perpendicular to the surface.

The movement of a camera, relative to an object, results in the change of both distance and orientation, which assist in determining the shape of that object. Determining the shape plays a significant role in object recognition rather than in manipulation tasks, as the significant cues provided by color, texture, and shape of the object helps in identifying the object and classify them into specific classes.

Speech Recognition

Speech is an important medium for communication between humans and is vital for human and machine communication. Mapping of the digitally encoded acoustic signal to a string of words is known as speech recognition. The limitations of this system prevent its extensive usage. The process of mapping from the acoustic signal to an interpretation of the meaningful sentence is called speech understanding. The acoustic sound signals are characterized in terms of features like amplitude and frequency. A basic understanding system fetches the most likely strings of words and passes them directly to the analyzer, whereas some understanding systems use a more complex control structure to select all the possible word interpretations so that understanding tasks would be successful even if some single words are indistinguishable. The grammar used in the speech recognition process is called perplexity. It counts the number of words that can legally appear next in the input. For example, in the case of telephone numbers, it measures only ten numbers.

Signal Processing in Speech Recognition

An electric current is produced when the sound waves hit the microphone. This electric current is then passed to an analog-to-digital converter, which in turn yields the digital information of the analog sound waves. Sampling rate and quantization factor are the two features of the sound waves which are used in determining the number of bits in digital information. Below given are the major steps in speech signal processing:

- Group the sample signals to larger blocks called frames. This helps to detect the appearance of variation in the frequency by analyzing the whole frame.

- Differentiate each frame based on various features of the sound signals.

- Perform the vector quantification in speech signals. If there are n features in a frame, it is possible to view the points in n-dimensional space. Vector quantification splits the n-dimensional space into say, 100 regions labeled C1 through C100. This helps in representing each frame with a single label, i.e., one byte per frame.

Even though the speech recognition is not fully accurate, there has been renewed interest in integrating speech recognition and natural language processing. Most modern speech systems are learning systems. These systems modify themselves by accepting a wide range of sample inputs and interpretations to enhance their ability to transform speech signals into appropriate words.

Perception enhances the capability of Artificial Intelligence to deal with real-world problems. It plays a vital role in Robotics as it aids in object localization, segmentation, and recognition. Perception is not a comprehensive, objective process; there are choices to be made. It is a result of experience evoked by a set of behaviors and predispositions. Advances in the concept of Perception have led to the progress of Robotics in a substantial manner.

Chapter 8

Implementation of PCA
and LDA in Python

Nowadays, every domain a large number of data are generated in machine learning applications such as text mining, computer vision and biomedical. So now, it's important to know how to utilize these large scale data. The large data contains noisy, redundant and irrelevant data. To reduce these data using dimensionality reduction method creates a new combination of attributes is called Feature extraction. Here I am using some techniques to reduce a large set of variables to a small set.

Introduction to Artificial Intelligence (AI)

- Artificial Intelligence (AI) is a method of building software or system behave smartly as human behave, i.e., computer-controlled robot

- This is achieved by analyzing human behavior like deciding on problem-solving, thinking, or learning leads to develop intelligent systems.

Goals of AI

To build expert systems: The systems that can offer intelligent advice, behavior, learn, explain, and demonstrate its users.

To execute human skills in systems: Generating machines that can think like humans.

Machine Learning: Machine Learning is the own learning technique by machine without the help of others programmed. It is an application of AI that provides a quality improvement process and extends the capability without human involvement.

With machine learning, things can be done more quickly and efficiently. The key factor which increased the importance of machine learning are:

Data Availability: Today, digital data is generated in huge amounts thanks to smart devices and IoT. Machine learning algorithms can analyze data and easily make intelligent decisions.

Computation Power: With the increase in computation power, current hardware can store and analyze data and perform a massive amount of computation in real-time.

What is the UCI Repository?

The UCI Machine Learning Repository is a collection of various databases for machine learning problems, domain theories, and data generators. It is hosted and maintained by the Center for Machine Learning and Intelligent Systems at the University of California, Irvine. David Aha created it as a graduate student at UC Irvine. Here I am using the IRIS dataset, which contains 150 number of instances and 4 number of attributes/features.

To download the dataset from the UCI Repository, follow the below steps.

Open UCI repository → Then click on view all data set(top right corner) → Select the dataset which one you want to download → Click on data folder link → Click on data → Copy all the text and paste on the excel sheet → Arrange the excel.

What is Principal Component Analysis (PCA)?

This section majorly targets audiences who are interested in understanding the basics of Principal component analysis (PCA). PCA plays a very important role in dimensionality reduction when your dataset has a large number of columns. PCA helps identify the columns that can be removed or combined with other columns to create newer dimensions of data. This tutorial will help understand the basics of PCA, how it is calculated, and what it does to a dataset. This tutorial will not provide detailed information on what is Eigenvalues and what is Kaiser Rule, because those are beyond the scope of basics.

PCA is a linear transformation technique that allows the data to transfer from higher dimensional space to lower-dimensional space or principal component analysis is selecting the fewer data from large dimensionality data set, which reduces the noisy, redundant and irrelevant data.

It is extracting relevant information from confusing, irrelevant data sets. It also removes the class labels and using unsupervised learning.

Goals:

1. PCA analysis is to identify patterns in high dimensional data.

2. PCA detects the correlation between variables.

3. It attempts to reduce the noise, higher dimensionality.

Output of PCA1:

[[11 0 0]

[0 12 1]

[0 1 5]]

Accuracy 0.9333333333333333

Output of PCA2:

[[11 0 0]

[0 10 3]

[0 2 4]]

Accuracy 0.8333333333333334

Here we see that the accuracy of PCA1 is 93.33% which is greater than the accuracy of PCA2 is 83.33%.

Basics of Principal Component Analysis

Principal Component Analysis is a concept of reducing the dimensions of the given data, thereby speeding up your learning algorithm and effective visualization of data. We would be taking only the first part mentioned, i.e., speeding up the learning algorithm. The learning algorithm can be linear regression, logistic regression, clustering or even neural networks.

Let us take a sample dataset – IOT.csv, which has 21 columns. Twenty columns of sensor data and the target column is Temperature. The dataset provides information about values captured by each sensor at a particular temperature and our purpose is to cluster the information based on the temperature range. The temperature ranges from 100 degrees Celsius to 700 degrees Celsius.

Sample Dataset can be seen below

Sensor 1	Sensor 2	Sensor 3	....	Sensor 18	Sensor 19	Sensor 20	Te mp
- 6.11005 61	- 7.26459 92	3.35934 97	....	- 6.49229 76	- 3.89810 77	- 6.95174 99	42 8
- 3.02979 15	- 1.56389 49	3.35962 45	....	- 3.82229 95	- 1.33075 19	- 5.29090 15	34 7
- 1.60769 58	- 1.26811 55	4.25694 5	....	- 6.90966 69	0.12504 99	- 4.69445 26	34 8
- 0.33055 72	5.20782 63	2.99225	....	4.85025 89	7.84360 47	6.22819 57	12 5
8.53415 39	7.34579 06	0.41990 75	....	2.26169 43	9.68115 27	2.92429 81	21 9

The dataset has 10000 rows and 21 columns. Since the dataset is huge, it is not provided here and a sample can be seen above. All the values provided in the above table are not real values, but just sample and imaginary values.

Import Libraries

The first step in any machine learning program in python is to import the necessary libraries like pandas, numpy, seaborn, etc.

The libraries can be imported like below

```
from sklearn.decomposition import PCA
import pandas as pd
import numpy as np
import seaborn as sns
import matplotlib.pyplot as plt
%matplotlib inline
```

Read Data from the File

Once the required libraries are imported, read the dataset into the file using pandas. Since this is a .csv file, we can use the read_csv method to read the contents of the file.

```
mydata = pd.read_csv("IOT.csv")
```

Once the above line of code is executed, it creates a data frame by name "mydata" and stores all the values from the file into the data frame.

Validate and Prepare Imported Data

You can use functions like head (), sample () to check whether the data is imported into the data frame.

> *mydata.head(5) – will print the first five values*
>
> *mydata.sample(5) – will print five random values from the dataframe.*

Check whether the data has any null or empty values. If so, either drop them or fill them with any of the preferred central tendency value (mean, median or mode)

mydata.fillna(<<mean>>) – this will fill all the NA values with mean.

Any dataset will have a dependent column whose output depends on other independent columns. The purpose of a machine learning algorithm is to predict this dependent column if you feed it values from independent columns. In IOT.csv, the dependent column is the Temperature, and the sensor data are the independent columns.

The cardinal rule of any dataset is that the correlation between independent variables should be as low as possible, whereas the correlation between each of the independent variables with the dependent variable should be as high as possible.

Check for correlation between columns, and accordingly, you can drop or modify columns.

> *mydata.corr() – will provide you the correlation quotient between all columns.*

156

Remember that just because a data appears normal, it doesn't mean that the data is indeed normalized data. You will have to check every column carefully before passing the data to the model for evaluation.

Use matplotlib or seaborn to do a pair plot and check the distribution of each column in the dataframe.

sns.pairplot(mydata)

The graph can show you whether the data is normally distributed or not. If it is not normally distributed, then employ normalization on the data using functions like ZScore or StandardScaler or MinMaxScaler. These can be imported from scikit-learn packages.

From sklearn.preprocessing import StandardScaler

Sc = StandardScaler

mydata_temp = mydata.pop('Temperatures') #pop the target column

mydata = sc.fit_transform(mydata)

At this stage your data is ready for principal component analysis.

Principal Component Analysis

When a correlation between columns is performed, it gives you independent correlation values for each column. There are cases where a column might have a very low correlation with the dependent column, but when paired with other columns, they can make a very good prediction on the dependent column.

Unless you are an expert in the domain on which the data set operates, it is very difficult to determine a column and its importance with respect to predicting targets. In the given example, if you are not a thermal or electrical engineer, you may not know which sensors are vital to determine the temperatures in a given range. So it becomes imperative that as a data scientist, you will have to work with multiple experts and make decisions accordingly.

Eigen Values and Kaiser Rule

The Eigenvalues and Kaiser Rule helps in finding out the total number of components that can be taken for consideration as part of PCA.

We will not go deep into what Eigenvalues and Kaiser Rule are all about. This article will just show you how to use the same.

Once the data set is ready, calculate the covariance of the data set by processing the data set as below

cov-matrix = np.cov(mydata)

The above line will give you the covariance matrix associated with the dataset. Once the covariance matrix is calculated, go ahead and calculate the Eigenvalues and Eigenvectors as below

eig_vals, eig_vecs = np.linalg.eig(cov-matrix)

 # Here eig_vals is the eigenvalue and the eig-vecs is the eigenvector

Now print the eigenvalues and see how many components have a value greater than 1.

For example, eig_vals = [1.4523346, 1.3254326, 1.2945346, 1.1298765, 0.4532987, 0.3332341, 0.23235354, 0.1243643, 0.03423423, 0.0078786, 0.0003432, 0.0000876]

In the above-given eigenvalues, as per Kaiser rule, you can notice there are just four components greater than one among the 12 components. So, we can safely assume that PCA can be effectively executed using several components as four.

Execute PCA

Import PCA from sklearn as below and use the function fit_transform() to transform mydata data set from 20 components to 4 components.

> *From sklearn.decomposition import PCA*
>
> *Pca = PCA (n_components = 4)*
>
> *my_transformed_data = Pca.fit_transform(mydata)*

The resulting my_transformed_data shall have only 4 components instead of 20 sensor component values. This way, it is clear that PCA has helped in reducing the dimensions from 20 to 4.

The resulting dataset, my_transformed_data, can then be passed into any models for further analysis.

Let us take a sample example of KMeans clustering. Since this document is all about PCA, we will not be going into details of KMeans and how optimal K values are calculated.

> *From sklearn.clusters import KMeans*

Kmeans = KMeans(k = 5)

Kmeans.fit(my_transformed_data)

From the above lines of code, we can see that KMeans clustering is applied not on the dataset, but the transformed dataset by PCA.

What is a Linear Discriminant Analysis (LDA)?

Linear Discriminant Analysis (LDA) is a linear transformation technique; a supervised algorithm seeks to reduce dimensionality. It is a very useful method for extracting relevant information from confusing data sets. The main idea is to find a projection to a line so that samples from the different classes are well separated.

Goals:

1. Selecting Eigenvectors from the dataset.

2. Arrange these in scatter matrix.

3. It provides k-dimensional data from d-dimensional dataset.

Output:

[[11 0 0]

[0 13 0]

[0 0 6]]

Accuracy: 1.0

Here we see that the LDA achieved an accuracy of 100%, which is greater than the accuracy achieved with PCA, i.e., 93.33%.

Therefore, LDA always performs better than PCA.

Chapter 9

Python Key Points for Deep Learning

One should be familiar with the basics of Python, which includes ideas about the Datatypes in python, especially Lists, Sets, Dictionary, Tuple, etc. Also, one should have a basic idea about OOPS in python. This is not an introductory chapter to python but a reference chapter containing a list of important concepts and functions in python needed to get a mastery Deep Learning. The concepts are explained with simple examples to get the basic idea of what they are. The concepts can be combined together to build powerful constructs and have to be practiced for comfort. I would suggest working on different problems to understand how these concepts fit on one another.

Concepts and Functions in Python for Deep Learning

Lambda: Lambda expressions are basically anonymous functions that can be used independently by assigning them to variables, in which case they would no longer be anonymous and by processing them into utilities like a map, reduce, filter, zip, etc. functions which take in functions as input arguments.

The general syntax of a lambda function is quite simple:

lambda argument_list: expression

For example:

>   f = lambda a, b, c : a + b + c
>   >>> f(10, 11, 12)
>   33

The above is synonymous with:

>   def f(a, b, c):
>   return a + b + c

The use of lambda expressions is to enable a programmer to write simple, short anonymous functions that can be easily used in other utilities without the need to define separate functions for those tasks. Even logical expressions can be embedded in lambda expression as below:

>   G = lambda a: 'large' if a > 15 else 'small'
>   >>> G(22)
>   'large'

Map: Map is another important function in Python. Map is used basically to apply a function to an iterable (list, set, dictionary, tuple, etc.). The syntax of the map function is:

map(fun, iter)

e.g.

l = [2, 3, 6]

out = map(lambda x:x**x, l)

>>> out

<map object at 0x035E6A50>

Now, as you can see, the output when printed prints map object, that's because the map does not return as a list/tuple/other input iterable, but a map object to be cast into any iterable desired.

For the above, if we use

>>> print(list(out))

[4, 27, 46656]

Map can also be used for operation on multiple iterables as below:

>>> l = [1, 2, 3]

>>> m = [4, 5, 6]

>>> n = [7, 8, 9]

>>> out = map(lambda x, y, z : x + y + z, l, m, n)

>>> print(list(out))

[12, 15, 18]

Reduce: Reduce is a simple function part of module functool from python3. What the function does is that it first applies a function on the first two elements of an iterable and then continuously applies the function by using the result of the last application as one argument and a new element from the list as another, till all the elements are exhausted. The syntax of the reduce function is below:

reduce(func, seq)

e.g.

>>> reduce(lambda x, y: x + y, range(1, 11))

55

The sum of 1 to 10

>>> reduce(lambda x, y: x if x > y else y, [2, 5, 6, 1, 8, 7])

8

Max number in a list

Filter: Filter is another of a functional utility in python. The Filter function just like map and reduce function takes in a function as an argument and an iterable as another argument and returns the element that satisfies the function (which means the function returns true) provided in the first argument. The function, like map, gives out a filter object which can be again inserted into the required iterable output. The syntax of the function is:

filter(func, seq)

e.g.

>>> list(filter(lambda x:x <0, [-5, 2, -3, 1, 0, -4]))

[-5, -3, -4]

Zip: Zip is a very useful utility in python, which takes two iterables as input and merges (individual merged unit is usually a tuple) them to return a zip object which again can be cast into another iterable datatype. Now, if the no of elements in both the input iterables is not the same, the zip function would stop when the shorter iterable is exhausted. The syntax for zip function is:

Zip(seq1, seq2)

> e.g.
> >>> a = [1, 2, 3]
> >>> b = [4, 5, 6]
> >>> ab = list(zip(a, b))
> >>> ab
> [(1, 4), (2, 5), (3, 6)]

Now, once zipped, the output can also be unzipped using the following syntax:

Zip(*seq)

> e.g.
> >>> c, d = zip(*ab)
> >>> c
> (1, 2, 3)
> >>> d
> (4, 5, 6)

Sorted: sorted() is a very useful function to sort any type of sequence object. The output of this function will always be a **list** (even though the input can be Tuple, list, dictionary, etc.). The syntax is as below:

sorted(iterable, key(optional), reverse(optional))

Here, key can be a value or a function. For example I would like to sort a python dictionary using this function

e.g.

```
>>> a = {'b':4, 'a':2, 'c':3}
>>> sorted(a)
['a', 'b', 'c']
```

Now,

Let's say we have to sort the dictionary using value, we will be using the key parameter for this

```
>>> dict(sorted(a.items(), key = lambda x:x[1]))
{'a': 2, 'c': 3, 'b': 4}
```

Now, the last segment of the syntax Reverse is used to reverse the order of the normal output, like:

```
>>> dict(sorted(a.items(), key = lambda x:x[1], reverse = True))
{'b': 4, 'c': 3, 'a': 2}
```

Join: Join is another very useful function in python. This utility is very useful when converting a list to string in a very easy way. The syntax is as below:-

string_name.join(iterable)

e.g.

```
>>> " ".join(["this", "is", "python"])
```

'this is python'

Range and Enumerate: These two are also very useful utility functions in python. The range is kind of the most used function in python. They are listed together as they are similar.

- Range(n) generates range object, which, when casting to a list, would give a list starting from 0 to n-1, which is very useful in for loops.

e.g.

>>> list(range(8))

[0, 1, 2, 3, 4, 5, 6, 7]

There is also an alternate syntax of the range, which is **range(I,n)**. Here I denote the starting point of the range. E.g.

>>> list(range(1,8))

[1, 2, 3, 4, 5, 6, 7]

Enumerate(seq), on the other hand, takes input, not an integer but a seq object like list, Tuple, etc. and generates a list/tuple of tuples where every element would be a tuple constructed from each element from the list and an integer starting from 0.

E.g.

>>> a = [10, 20, 30, 40, 50]

>>> list(enumerate(a))

[(0, 10), (1, 20), (2, 30), (3, 40), (4, 50)]

Other syntax is **enumerate(seq,start)**, where one can specify the start of the integer to be coupled with the list values. For e.g.

>>> list(enumerate(a, 11))

$$[(11, 10), (12, 20), (13, 30), (14, 40), (15, 50)]$$

Any and All: These are very helpful validation functions that usually work on iterators. Basically, they take an input, which is a sequence of Boolean values and return true/false if any of them is true or if all of them are false. The syntax is:

any(seq)/all(seq)

For example, the below statement returns true if all of the lists of integers are positive and if any of them is a palindrome integer.

>>> list1 = [21, 50, 19, 35, 91, 215]

print(all(a>0 for a in list1) and any(str(b) == str(b)[::-1] for b in list1))

*args and **kwargs:

Usual definition of a function in python is:

def func(arg1, arg2):

   print(arg1, arg2)

Now, the above function will always take two arguments, which, if not provided, will result in a Type error. The arguments can be supplied in two ways in python; one is the normal way as below:

>>> func("Hello", "World")

Hello World

Also, another way the arguments that could be supplied is in a keyworded manner as below:

>>> func(arg2 = "Hello", arg1 = "World")

World Hello

Now, let's say we want to make the above function flexible enough to take any no. of arguments, then we use the *args and **kwargs arguments. Here, the name args and kwargs doesn't matter, what matters is the indicator parameter * and **. Defining any function as below specifies that it can take a list of arguments:

def test(*argx):

　　for arg in argx:

　　　print(arg)

Now, when calling it using test("this", "is", "a", "test"). The output is:

this

is

a

test

Now, ** is similar but a tad bit different from * argument. The ** takes in a keyword set of arguments (like a dictionary) as below:

def test1(**argx):

　for arg in argx.items():

169

print(arg)

test1(arg1 = "this", arg2 = "is", arg3 = "a", arg4 = "test")

('arg1', 'this')

('arg2', 'is')

('arg3', 'a')

('arg4', 'test')

Comprehensions (List, Set, and Dictionary): Comprehensions are another very useful concept, where we can build sequences from other sequences. Comprehensions are very powerful in a sense because just through one construct, the reason we will see soon. The syntax of comprehension is below; the set and dictionary comprehension is also very similar.

The syntax consists of 4 parts: [see below example]

- Input sequence = this contains the initial sequence using which we are building the new sequence. E.g. range(1, 11)

- Variable = this is representing members of the input sequence. E.g., for x in

- Predicate expression = this optional and is used to filter out data from the input sequence. E.g. if x % 2 == 0

- Output expression = finally, the output formula which transforms the selected data from the input sequence to the desired output. E.g., x**2

E.g.

To build a list that would have squares of all even numbers from 1 to 10 would be:

>>> **[x**2 for x in range(1, 11) if x % 2 == 0]**

[4, 16, 36, 64, 100]

Now, if you see carefully the above list can also be created by using the following expression:

>>> **list(map(lambda x:x**2,filter(lambda x:x%2 == 0, range(1, 11))))**

[4, 16, 36, 64, 100]

So basically, list comprehension is combining the facilities of a map, filter as well as a lambda expression in one expression, making this technique a powerful one.

Similarly, examples of Set and Dictionary comprehensions are given below:

For the set comprehension example, I am constructing a set from the below list in a way that only the first letter of each element is in uppercase.

abc = ["Mary", "John", "Pat", "Lucky", "MARY", "mary", "JOHN", "Chang"]

>>> {x[0].upper() + x[1:].lower() for x in abc if len(x) > 2 }

{'Mary', 'John', 'Pat'}

Now, let's see an example of dictionary comprehension:-

>>> bla = {'abc': 10, 'ABC': 5, 'CDE': 15, 'cde': 10}

>>> {x.lower():bla.get(x.lower()) + bla.get(x.upper()) for x in bla}

{'abc': 15, 'cde': 25}

Generator Expressions and Functions: Let's take an expression for example after we have already looked in to list comprehensions:

(x**2 for x in range(1, 11) if x % 2 == 0)

If you run this at the python console the output would be:

<generator object <genexpr> at 0x030D1E10>

So, basically what we have created here is called generator expression, the only difference between this and list/set/dictionary comprehension is the brackets (). If you see carefully, you will find that comprehensions always use [] (for list) or {} (for set or dictionary).

So, list comprehensions are nothing but, generator expressions converted into a list. But when these conversions happen, an interesting thing occurs. See, a generator expression is nothing but a generator object, which contains no data and can be traversed using for loop or converted into list/set/dictionary (using comprehension), and only at that time these expressions generate data, for lists/set/dictionary, the data is stored in memory.

Like generator expressions, generator functions can be created as below:

E.g.

def abc(n):

...   **for x in range(1, n+1):**

...   **if x % 2 == 0:**

...   **yield x**2**

>>> list(abc(10))

[4, 16, 36, 64, 100]

Here, a special keyword **yield** is used to convert a normal function to a generator function.

Significance of _ in python:

_ is a very widely used literal in Python, especially in OOPS in python, so trying to list a few of the uses and differences I could find in python is given below:-

1.Standalone _:

Standalone _ can be used for different reasons. If used in the python console, it will give the last result, for example:

>>> a = 5

```
>>> a

5

>>> _

5

>>>
```

Standalone _ can also be used for ignoring values of variables we would not be using like:-

```
>>> for _ in range(5):
...     print("ABC")
...
ABC
ABC
ABC
ABC
ABC
```

2. Single _ After a variable name:

Python has its own reserved keyword that cannot be used as a variable name, as below:

```
>>> class = []
  File "<stdin>", line 1
    class = []
         ^
```

SyntaxError: invalid syntax

So, one can easily use them like:

class_ = []

3.Single _ Before a variable/method name:

Using an underscore before a variable/method name indicates the programmer that the variable or method is for internal use only. Now, if used within a class, import * from class does not import the methods starting with _. But normal import does import them so they are of not much reliable and can be only used as a convention.

4.Leading Double _ before variable of method:

Now, naming a variable or method with leading __, causes an interesting phenomenon called name mangling in Python. See, when we specify __ before any variable/method name in python, Python interpreter renames the variable/method to _classname__method/variable name as below:

```
>>> class abc:
...    def __check():
...            print("double underscore")
...
>>> b = abc()
```

Dir function shows details of methods and variables available under the object.

Counter and orderedDict from collection library:

Python has innumerable utility functions for ease of use of programming. There are many libraries in python like Itertools, Collection, functools, etc. I would suggest going through them to get your own set of favorite functions. I am mentioning here two very useful must know the functions that are found in the collection framework.

Counter:

The counter is useful because it takes the input as a list and returns the count of unique items in the list is a dictionary pattern.

For e.g.

> myList = [1, 1, 2, 3, 4, 5, 3, 2, 3, 4, 2, 1, 2, 3]
>
> **>>> Counter(myList)**
>
> Counter({2: 4, 3: 4, 1: 3, 4: 2, 5: 1})

OrderedDict:-

It is a type of dictionary that will remember all the ordering in the order of their insertion. Suppose a new value is overwriting the currently existing value, then the order of insertion will not change and will be the same only. Please note it might not work in Python 3.6 as it maintains the order for some cases. Therefore, it is suggested to use this approach in Python 3.5 version.

Even when equality is checked **between 2 normal dictionary**, it only checks whether all keys and values between those 2 dictionaries are same as below:-

> >>> dict1 = {}
>
> >>> dict1['a'] = 'A'
>
> >>> dict1['b'] = 'B'

```
>>> dict1['c'] = 'C'
>>> dict2 = {}
>>> dict2['c'] = 'C'
>>> dict2['b'] = 'B'
>>> dict2['a'] = 'A'
>>> dict1
{'a': 'A', 'b': 'B', 'c': 'C'}
>>> dict2
{'c': 'C', 'b': 'B', 'a': 'A'}
>>> dict1 == dict2
True
```

But, OrderedDict takes in consideration the order too, as below:

```
>>> from collections import OrderedDict
>>> ord_dict1 = OrderedDict()
>>> ord_dict2 = OrderedDict()
>>> ord_dict1['a'] = 'A'
>>> ord_dict1['b'] = 'B'
>>> ord_dict1['c'] = 'C'
>>> ord_dict2['c'] = 'C'
>>> ord_dict2['b'] = 'B'
>>> ord_dict2['a'] = 'A'
>>> ord_dict2 == ord_dict1
False
```

Use of Natural Language Processing in Deep Learning

We often come across terms like Artificial Intelligence, Machine Learning, and Deep Learning in computer journals, computer magazines, and news. What are these technologies? The answer is simple, and if we go deep down inside to comprehend its meaning, it is also complicated at the same time. It can be described as a zone of computer science which tries to embed intelligence inside machines so that these machines can predict or perceive the environment and use the intelligence to take actions that turn up in the efficient consequences. The best examples of Artificial Intelligence are Computer Games such as Chess, Brick Arranging or even Cricket and soccer, etc. The amazing thing is when you introduce a new move in the game, the computer automatically introduces a move to beat you up.

There are several branches of Deep Learning. But one of the most important is Natural Language Processing.

Natural Language Processing

It is an area of Deep Learning which focuses on human and computer interactions. Precisely, it emphasizes the field of computer science as well as linguistics. The elements of human language are formalized and are coded in such a way that the machine itself performs tasks such as translation, sentence correction, or even the motive of the speech, etc.

What if a machine performs the following tasks?

Interpret a sentence from One Language to Other.

Derive parts of speech of different words in a sentence.

Ask a question, and the program gives you the answer.

Determine the textual representation of a verbal conversation.

These are some of the particular areas of research in Natural Language Processing.

The computational Techniques which are used are of immense importance in Natural Language Processing. It is very much necessary to choose a particular technique from a wide range of techniques to do proper language analysis. It is very important to bring in the texts which are actually used in human languages under research; the clear picture is the text should not be constructed for the analysis. Rather it should be taken from actual human languages.

Aim of NLP

The main aim of NLP (Natural Language Processing) is to basically develop a Program through which human-like language processing is possible. However, this aim has yet not been achieved but researches are still on in a positive direction in different scenarios pertaining to language processing. Those researches have been going on for achieving the following goals (also mentioned above):

- Interpret a sentence from One Language to the Other Language.

- Derive parts of speech of different words in a sentence.

- Ask a question, and the program gives you the answer

- Determine the textual representation of a verbal conversation.

Some progress has been made in the first three, while the fourth one still shows up as a complex task to accomplish for the researchers.

The Objectives of NLP are very much complicated if we try to have a deep understanding of them. For example, if we try to develop a program that can answer any question which the human asks it. Now think of the complexities involved in it. First, the complete structure of the program should be like the human brain i.e., the program should be able to manipulate according to the question and provide the user with an answer. The Questions can be thrown as "Who is the president of United States of America?" the answer to this question is quite simple for the program to understand but if a question is like "What is your perception of Success?" the answer to this involves deep thinking and also different types of mindsets and different kind of manipulations which only a human brain can do. Hence, it is considered as an important research topic for the researchers.

History

The history of the Natural Language Processing dates back to the early 1950s when the experiment to impersonate a human conversation was held. From then, several types of research have been conducted to achieve the objectives of real language processing. Some very successful works began and got completed in the 1960s. During the 1970s, a natural language processing system with restricted vocabularies was developed. Till the 1980s, the NLP systems were based on a restricted set of rules, regulations, and vocabularies. But a revolution began with the development of machine learning. Though natural language processing has always been a complex phenomenon, effort has been made and is going on to achieve the objective completely. However, to achieve the objective completely, an algorithm must be created, which completely resembles the working of a human mind, which is considered to be the most complicated task in this industry.

Constitution

NLP encompasses two things:

1. Natural Language Understanding (NLU)

When the human language is fed as an input to the NLP system, NLUs task is to comprehend and, based on the comprehension, generate adequate reasoning.

2 Natural Language Generation (NLG)

It is generally referred to as a subfield of the Natural Language Processing and is prominently used for language generation

Levels of Natural Language Processing

NLP_usually_has five levels. Let's have a brief look at them:

- Morphological and Lexical Analysis: The vocabulary in a language constitutes its lexicon, whereas morphology pertains to the identification or description of these words in a paragraph or a text.

- Syntactic Analysis: The words in a sentence which constitute the sentence are checked here whether they fit grammatically inside the sentence otherwise they would be rejected by the NLP system

- Semantic Analysis: In this stage, the possible meanings of the sentence are derived in terms of the context. It takes the output of the syntactic analysis stage as input and derives meanings.

- Discourse Integration: In this stage, it is checked whether the meaning of a word depends upon the sentences preceding or following it.

- Pragmatic Analysis: In this stage, the answer is given to the question, "What is meant in a sentence?" For this, knowledge of external communication is strictly necessary. The objective is to determine the purpose of a sentence or precisely, the purpose of the sentence. For E.g., "Could you bring me some water?" should be interpreted as a request.

Research Areas

Following are the areas in which the researches are going on to achieve the aim of NLP:

- Speech Processing: This area mainly focuses on speech recognition. One more aspect of this research is text-to-speech conversion.

- Segmentation of Speech: To break the speech of a person into words and analyze the context. A subtask of Speech Processing.

- Title Recognition: If a chunk of text is given to the program, then the program itself determines the title of the text.

- Language Conversion: If a sentence is given in Russian, it should be able to convert the sentence into Spanish or any desired language.

- Summarization: If a large paragraph or an essay is given a proper summary of the paragraph or essay gets generated pertaining to the context.

- Answering Questions: This area focuses on answering the human questions. As mentioned above, the answers to questions like "What is the capital of the USA?" is easy, but the answer to "What is your Perception of success?" is pretty hard.

Chapter 9

Robot Framework with Python

The robot framework is an open-source keyword-driven test automation framework. Pekka Clark provided its basic idea in his master thesis. This framework is implemented using python and also runs on Jython and iron python. The main benefit of this framework is platform-independent and support working with almost all the applications. Robot framework support different format of test case files are HTML, TSV, or Plain text. The robot framework test also generates HTML format result reports and logs after a complete run of tests.

Features of Robot Framework

For selecting any automation framework features, benefits over other frameworks are considered. Below are the features and benefits of the robot framework:

- Platform Independent: Robot framework is supported for all widely used platform windows, UNIX, MAC, and test cases created in robot framework are also platform-independent.

Test cases created in one platform can be easily used with other platforms.

- Open Source: The robot framework is an open-source framework, and it is maintained regularly. The robot framework is created under the Nokia Siemens network and released under the Apache 2.0 license. So it can be used freely.

- Suitableness: Robot framework provides support for almost all applications, tools. It provides support of selenium for web testing, Java GUI testing, running processes, Telnet, and SSH.

- Reporting: Robot framework generates its own reports and logs in HTML format after a run of the test. It also has one tool, "rebot," which can be used to generate reports and logs from XML output files.

- Ease: Robot framework test cases can be created in a text file format, HTML, TSV. So, it is very easy to create test cases using this framework and created test cases that are easy to read.

- Extendibility: Robot framework supports several standards, external and other libraries like builtin, operating system, processes, screenshot, telnet, strings, dialogs, Remote, Collections, XML, DateTime, Android, Selenium, Appium, FTP, Database, MongoDB, iOS, watir, remote. These libraries provide keywords for writing test cases of different functionalities. The robot framework also supports the creation of user-defined libraries by using Python or Jython or iron python for supporting some application-related functionality keyword. So, robot framework functionality can be extended easily by using standard libraries with external and user-defined libraries.

- Gherkin language support: Robot framework test cases can also be written in gherkin language format using given, when, then. So robot framework supports test case writing using a BDD approach.

- Reusability: The robot framework uses a keyword-driven approach. So, the created keyword can also be used more than one time for performing the same functionality with different data/scenarios.

- Maintenance: The maintenance cost of the robot framework is also less than other frameworks, as it is a keyword-driven framework. So on changes in functionality, it will require a change in a library function. Minimum or No changes in test cases or test suite will be required.

- Continuous integration: Robot framework also support run with Jenkins and Team city Ci tool.

- Support: The robot framework has an active community for contributors and its bug/issue resolution work.

So robot framework is a highly considerable framework that can be used freely and easily with a different application.

Framework Architecture

In the robot framework, test data is parsed to the created Robot framework functionality keywords. Keywords call Test library function, and library function can be built-in or created using Python or Jython (JVM) or iron python (.NET). Library function interacts with an application under test. So the robot framework helps in maintaining abstraction with the help of a keyword-driven framework in the developed scripts and easy to reuse generated keyword.

Selecting Python/Jython/IronPython

Jython (JVM) and iron python (.NET) are the different implementations of python. The selection of Python/Jython/IronPython for the creation of test libraries depends on application under test. Jython can be used for java based application, and iron python can be used for .net based application. In this section, python is considered for the creation of libraries for keywords.

Example:

For working on robot framework, compatible python, and robot framework should be installed on the system. Consider an example for comparing (audit) OS and installed application details on the system:

System Under Test: Windows machine.

Test Tools: command prompt of windows machine.

Test Libraries: Test libraries are functions written in python. In python, the function begins with "def," followed by function name and parenthesis. Required arguments are passed within parenthesis.

In python, variables can be created without an explicit type declaration. Function code start with a colon and statement of codes are indented. For example, a library python file is created, windowsCmdOpearation.py.

Two modules are imported "os" and "subprocess."

- os module: It provides a way of using functionality related to an operating system like file open, read, write, changes directory. In the example open, write and close file functions are used.

- Open: This function can be used for opening a file.

Syntax: fileobject = open(filename, accessmode, buffering)

Arguments details:

- filename: It is the name or path of the file that is required to access.

- accessmode: this is the mode in which file should be required to open, i.e., Read (r), write (w), append (a), or combination (r+, a+, w+) or opening files read, write append in binary format (rb, wb, ab, rb+, wb+, ab+).

- buffering: It is used to set the buffer value in file opening.

- Write: This function can be used to write data in the opened file.

Syntax: fileobject.write(stringoutput)

stringoutput argument contains content to be written in the opened file.

- Close: This function can be used to close the opened file.

Syntax: fileobject.close()

- Subprocess module: It allows to start a new child process, connect to their input/output/error pipes and to get their return code. In the example "subprocess.Popen(args/cmd to run, <out/error pipe> <shell =true/false>)" interface and "Popen.communicate()" function are used.

- Subprocess.Popen(): It is used to call or run another command in the child process, the output of cmd or called process can be stored by passing PIPE for the stdout/stderr. "shell = true" in poepn specifies the default shell.

Syntax: popenobject = subprocess.Popen(args/cmd to run, <out/error pipe> <shell = true/false>)"

- Popen.communicate(): It returns a tuple of output and error details.

Syntax: (stdoutdatavar, stderrdatavar) = popenobject.communicate()

In the above example, two functions are created that can be used as library keyword.

windowsCmd():

- Function created for running commands passed as argument in "cmdTorun" on windows command prompt and storing result in a given text file passed as argument in "outputfilename."

- The "rsyncProcess" variable is used to store the output of cmd "supprocess.Popen(cmdTorun, stdout = subprocess.PIPE, shell = true)". So now, the rsyncProcess variable can be used for getting output and error by using communicate function.

- In the above example, "stdoutdata" and "stderrdata" are used to store output and error details. stderrdata will contain any value only if the cmd run process is executed with some error or failure.

- So if-else loop is used to check the status of error. If the error exists (value of stderrdata variable shouldn't be none), then an exception is raised by "raise exception(args)" command.

- In an else loop, if command passes successfully then "outputfilename" variable value is used to open/create a file for appending in binary format by "open(outputfilename, ab)," and the opened file is stored in variable "text_file." For writing data in the opened file "write" function is used and "stdoutdata" variable is used as an argument for storing output. "text_file.close()" is used to close the opened file.

compareResult():

- Function created for comparing two text files passed as arguments in "file1", "file2".

- In this function, the "Popen" interface is used for running command FC (for windows) for comparison of two files, and popen output is stored in variable rsyncProcess.

- Output and error details are stored in the "stdoutdata" and "stderrdata" variable by using command rsyncProcess.communicate.

- If an error exists, then an exception is raised by "raise exception(args)," and if no error exists in the file comparison, then "pass" print on screen by using "print("pass")".

For using this created library in the robot framework, the library should be present in the python library path or library path should be declared in an environment variable or complete absolute path can also be used for importing in robot framework test cases.

Test Data/Robot Framework

Test cases created using Plain text tab-separated syntax of robot framework.

- How to run a robot framework test suite:

In command prompt run following command:

pybot WindowsAudittest.txt

Subsequently, completing run it generates logs and report files: log.html, report.html, output.xml. Generated reports contain details of test execution time and it has a red background if there's a failure and green background if all test cases pass.

- For running one test in a test suite file.

  Syntax: pybot –t <test name> <test suite file name>

For e.g., pybot –t "Windows OS details audit" WindowsAudittest.txt

- Creating a test suite using the robot framework: In robot framework, a single text file is considered as a test suite; it can have multiple test cases. Robot framework test suite files contain different fields/tables i.e., Settings, Variables, and Test Cases.

  Settings: Used to import test libraries and to define Documentation of the test suite. In the above example, two test libraries are imported, and Documentation is given.

  Variables: Used to define variables that can be used in different test cases of the same test suite file. In the above example, two variables are created that can be used in test cases. In this ${CURDIR} is a built-in variable in the robot framework that can be used to denote the current directory.

Test Cases: Used to create multiple test cases from keywords of test libraries. In the above example, two test cases are created by using library keywords. In this example, different system commands are passed as data for run, and results are compared with template files.

Creating Custom Libraries for Robot Framework

In this section, we will see how to create custom libraries using the python language and how to associate it with the robot framework.

Need for Custom Libraries

Sometimes keywords/functionalities provided by the library may not be sufficient; in such cases, the user needs to create their own custom library and associate it to an existing test suite. In the Robot framework, users can create custom libraries using java, python.

Features

- User can include multiple libraries in one test suite.

- It provides the ability to customize success/failure messages in the report.

- The library, once created, can be called anywhere and any number of times in the test suite.

- Reusability of the library created.

Scenario 1

Taking Telephone Directory web application for this scenario. In this scenario, once the user searches with an employee ID, in the result folder, I am doing verification of employee name (String comparison Case sensitive and String comparison Case Insensitive). Since selenium library doesn't have inbuilt functions for string comparison, we have created a custom library using python language.

Scenario 2

Taking a web outlook application for this scenario. When the user launches this application, a windows dialog box pops up for authenticating the user. AutoIT can handle this kind of dialogs box. Using AutoIt, the user can create a .exe file that has actions performed on window controls. Using python, the user can call this .exe file anytime and any number of times as per requirement.

Scenario 1

The following are the steps for the same.

- Open Telephone Directory web app

- Search with an employee using employee ID

- Get Employee name form the application

- Verify Employee name (String comparison Case sensitive)

- Verify Employee name (String comparison Case Insensitive)

Code for String Comparison is Below

```python
import re

import os

import string

class Stringcompare:

    def StringcompareSensitive(self, str1, str2):

        flag = str1.find(str2)

        if flag >= 0 :

            print "'%s' is  matching with '%s'" % (str1, str2)

        elif flag == -1 :

            raise ValueError("'" + str1 + "' is  not matching  '" + str2 + "'")

    def StringcompareInsensitive(self, str1, str2):

        temp1 = str1.lower()

        temp2 = str2.lower()

        flag = temp1.find(temp2)

        if flag >= 0 :
```

```
            print "'%s' is  matching with '%s'" % (str1,
str2)

        elif flag == -1 :

        raise ValueError("'" + str1 + "' is not matching  '" +
str2 + "'")
```

The above code will be saved as .py format. To create a custom library, we need to execute .py files through the command prompt.

Below are Steps to Demonstrate .py files Execution

Open the command prompt and navigate to the folder containing .py file (code for the custom library) and select .py file and press enter.

Once the above step is done, then compiled python file is generated in .pyc format.

Now, the custom library is created and ready to use.so our next step is to incorporate this library to test suite along with other libraries.

Please Find the Below Code

```
    *** Settings ***

    Documentation              To demonstrate custom
    library creation

    Library        Selenium2Library              120s

    Library        Stringcompare
```

*** Test Cases ***

Testing the reqd

    Open Browser   internetexplorer

    Input Text
name=_ctl0:ContentPlaceHolder1:txtSearch ${abc}

    Click Element
id=_ctl0_ContentPlaceHolder1_lnkSearch

    ${xyz}   Get Text
id=_ctl0_ContentPlaceHolder1_gvEmployeeDetails
__ctl3_lblName

    Stringcomparesensitive ${xyz} Mary

    Stringcompareinsensitive ${xyz} Mary

As shown in above code two libraries are added, one is standard library which is Selenium2 Library for testing web applications and second is custom library Stringcompare.

Scenario 2

The following are the steps for the same.

- Open Web outlook Portal.

- The Windows dialog box is populated.

- Enter user credentials using a custom library in the dialog box.

- Verify whether the user is logged in.

- Sign Out.

- Close Browser.

Following is a Simple Python Code to Call .exe file:

```
import sys

import os

class CallExe:

  def Execute_exe_(self,name):

      try:

        os.system(name)

        print "'%s' is called" % (name)

      except Exception:

        raise ValueError("Exe is not called")
```

Now User Associates this Library to his Test Suite as Shown Below.

```
*** Settings ***

Documentation            TO handle Window popup

Library      Selenium2Library            60s

Library            CallExe

Library            AutoIt
```

Therefore, the Robot framework is simple enough to use it for building keyword-driven test automation and reusing the generated keywords in multiple test cases. Robot framework is easy to use for manual testers too, such as manual tester just need to be aware of the keyword of different functionality, and they can use keywords for creating test cases without any knowledge of OOPS or other programming languages.

Conclusion

So we have learned about the realms of deep learning from a beginner's perspective. We covered all the important chapters that are required to understand and implement Deep learning in your practical learning experience. I hope after reading this book, you will be able to easily differentiate between Deep learning and Machine learning. Also, you will be able to use neural networks for pattern recognition and speech recognition.

Moreover, the implementation of PCA in Python will give you the complete hands-on experience you need to understand deep learning. Lastly, we also covered the Robot framework for you. This book was created for a beginner's level and I hope you like it. We will also be releasing the intermediate level book on deep learning for those who want to dig deeper into it and solve more complex problems. Look forward to seeing you in the next book!

www.ingramcontent.com/pod-product-compliance
Lightning Source LLC
La Vergne TN
LVHW051230050326
832903LV00028B/2321